Scottish Football Supporters' Guide and Yearbook 2014

EDITOR
John Robinson

Twenty-first Edition

CONTENTS

British Library Cataloguing in Publication Data
A catalogue record for this book is available from the British Library

ISBN: 978-1-86223-270-9

72 St. Peter's Avenue, Cleethorpes, N.E. Lincolnshire, DN35 8HU, England

Web site www.soccer-books.co.uk
e-mail info@soccer-books.co.uk

Manufactured in the UK by 4edge Ltd.

FOREWORD

Due to the uncertainties which faced Scottish Football for 2012/2013 as a result of the upheaval caused by the liquidation of the original Rangers FC company, the season settled down very well after the first few weeks and reached a successful conclusion. The 'new' Rangers FC acquitted themselves well and were promoted as 3rd Division Champions, beginning their expected rise back towards the top division of Scottish football.

However, since the end of the 2012/2013 season, The Scottish Football League has, effectively, ceased to exist and the 30 clubs who were members of that League have now been absorbed by the Scottish Premier League into an organisation with the title of "The Scottish Professional Football League".

Furthermore, the senior echelons of Lowland Scottish Non-League football have been reorganised into a new 'Lowland League' which will be on a par with The Highland League. This new structure will provide a potential route into the Scottish Professional Football League at the end of the 2013/2014 season via a play-off between the champions of the Lowland League and the Highland League. As details of the new Lowland League had not been completely established when we went to press, we hope to include further details in future editions of our guide.

We wish to thank the club secretaries for their assistance in providing the information contained in this guide. We also wish to thank Bob Budd for the cover artwork.

If readers have up-to-date ground photographs which they wish us to consider for inclusion in a future edition, please contact us at the address on the facing page.

Additional copies of this guide can be obtained directly from us at the address shown on the facing page. Alternatively, orders may be placed securely via our web site – www.soccer-books.co.uk

Finally, we would like to wish our readers a happy and safe spectating season.

John Robinson
EDITOR

The Scottish Football Association

Founded

1873

Address

National Stadium, Hampden Park,
Mount Florida, Glasgow G42 9AY

Web Site

www.scottishfa.co.uk

Phone

(0141) 616-6000

Fax

(0141) 616-6001

HAMPDEN – SCOTLAND'S NATIONAL STADIUM

Opened: 1903
Location: Hampden Park, Mount Florida, Glasgow G42 9BA
Telephone Nº: (0141) 620-4000
Fax Number: (0141) 620-4001

Record Attendance: 150,239
(Scotland vs England, 17th April 1937)
Pitch Size: 115 × 75 yards
Ground Capacity: 52,063 (All seats)
Web Site: www.hampdenpark.co.uk

GENERAL INFORMATION

Car Parking: 536 spaces + 39 disabled spaces at Stadium
Coach Parking: Stadium Coach Park
Nearest Railway Station: Mount Florida and King's Park (both are 5 minutes walk)
Nearest Bus Station: Buchanan Street

DISABLED INFORMATION

Wheelchairs: Accommodated in disabled spectators sections at all levels in the South Stand, particularly levels 1 and 4 where special catering and toilet facilities are available.
Disabled Toilets: Available
Commentaries are available for the blind
Contact: (0141) 620-4000

Travelling Supporters' Information:
Routes: From the South: Take the A724 to the Cambuslang Road and at Eastfield branch left into Main Street and follow through Burnhill Street and Westmuir Place into Prospecthill Road. Turn left into Aikenhead Road and right into Mount Annan for Kinghorn Drive and the Stadium; From the South: Take the A77 Fenwick Road, through Kilmarnock Road into Pollokshaws Road then turn right into Langside Avenue. Pass through Battle Place to Battlefield Road and turn left into Cathcart Road. Turn right into Letherby Drive, right into Carmunnock Road and 1st left into Mount Annan Drive for the Stadium; From the North & East: Exit M8 Junction 15 and passing Infirmary on left proceed into High Street and cross the Albert Bridge into Crown Street. Join Cathcart Road and proceed South until it becomes Carmunnock Road. Turn left into Mount Annan Drive and left again into Kinghorn Drive for the Stadium.

The Scottish Professional Football League – The Scottish Premier League

Address
National Stadium, Hampden Park,
Mount Florida, Glasgow G42 9DE

Web Site www.scotprem.com

Phone (0141) 620-4140
Fax (0141) 620-4141

Clubs for the 2013/2014 Season

ABERDEEN FC

Founded: 1903 (**Entered League**: 1904)
Nickname: 'The Dons'
Ground: Pittodrie Stadium, Pittodrie Street, Aberdeen AB24 5QH
Ground Capacity: 21,421 (all seats)
Record Attendance: 45,061 (13th March 1954)
Pitch Size: 115 × 72 yards

Colours: Red shirts and shorts
Telephone Nº: (01224) 650400
Ticket Office: (01224) 631903
Fax Number: (01224) 644173
Web Site: www.afc.co.uk
E-mail: feedback@afc.co.uk

GENERAL INFORMATION

Car Parking: Beach Promenade, King Street and Golf Road
Coach Parking: At the rear of the Stadium in Golf Road car park (£10.00 charge)
Nearest Railway Station: Aberdeen (1 mile)
Nearest Bus Station: Aberdeen
Club Shop: At the ground
Opening Times: Monday to Saturday 9.00am to 5.00pm.
Telephone Nº: (01224) 642800 or 212797

GROUND INFORMATION

Away Supporters' Entrances & Sections:
Park Road entrance for the South Stand East

ADMISSION INFO (2013/2014 PRICES)

Adult Seating: £18.00 to £28.00
Under-12s Seating: £6.00 to £11.00
Senior Citizen/Under-18s/Students: £10.00 to £20.00
Programme Price: £2.50

DISABLED INFORMATION

Wheelchairs: 7 spaces available in the South Stand for away fans. 26 spaces in total for home fans
Helpers: One helper admitted per wheelchair
Prices: Free of charge for wheelchair disabled and helpers
Disabled Toilets: Available in the Richard Donald Stand, the Merkland Stand, in the Away Section and in a new toilet block at the Richard Donald Stand entrance
Contact: (01224) 631903 (Bookings are necessary)

Travelling Supporters' Information:
Routes: From the City Centre, travel along Union Street then turn left into King Street. The Stadium is about ½ mile along King Street (A92) on the right-hand side.

CELTIC FC

Founded: 1888 (**Entered League**: 1890)
Nickname: 'The Bhoys' 'The Hoops'
Ground: Celtic Park, Glasgow G40 3RE
Ground Capacity: 60,355 (All seats)
Record Attendance: 92,000 (1st January 1938)
Pitch Size: 115 × 74 yards

Colours: Green & White hooped shirts, White shorts
General Telephone N°: 0871 226-1888
General Fax Number: (0141) 551-8106
Ticket Office Number: 0871 226-1888
Web Site: www.celticfc.net

GENERAL INFORMATION

Car Parking: Limited on Matchdays to those with a Valid Car Park Pass. Otherwise, street parking
Coach Parking: Gallowgate, Fielden Street, Biggar Street and Nuneaton Street
Nearest Railway Station: Bellgrove (10 minutes walk)
Nearest Bus Stop: Outside of the ground
Club Shop: Superstore at Celtic Park. Also in Glasgow: 21 High Street; 215 Sauchiehall Street; 154 Argyle Street; Terminal 1, Glasgow Airport. Elsewhere: 5 West Blackhall Street, Greenock; 24 West Mall, The Plaza, East Kilbride Shopping Centre; 34 Frederick Street, Edinburgh; 74 Sylvania Way, The Clyde Shopping Centre, Clydebank; 72 Main Street, Coatbridge; Unit 26, The Thistle Centre, Stirling; 30/34 Ann Street, Belfast; 4/6 Bishop St., Derry; Unit 10, 125 Upper Abbey St., Dublin. Also in selected Debenhams outlets throughout Scotland and Ireland
Opening Times: Please contact the Superstore for details
Telephone N°: (0141) 551-4231 (Superstore)

GROUND INFORMATION

Away Supporters' Entrances & Sections:
Kinloch Street Turnstiles for the East Stand

ADMISSION INFO (2013/2014 PRICES)

Please contact the club for information about ticket pricing for the 2013/2014 season.

DISABLED INFORMATION

Wheelchairs: 141 spaces for home fans and 6 spaces for away fans in the North Stand and East Stand
Helpers: 144 helpers admitted in total
Prices: Please contact the club for information about ticket pricing for disabled supporters during the 2013/2014 season.
Disabled Toilets: 5 available in the North Stand, 2 in the East Stand and 3 in the South West Stand
Contact: 0871 226-1888 (Bookings are necessary)

Travelling Supporters' Information:
Routes: From the South and East: Take the A74 London Road towards the City Centre, Celtic Park is on the right about ½ mile past the Belvidere Hospital and the ground is clearly visible; From the West: Take the A74 London Road from the City Centre and turn left about ½ mile past Bridgeton Station.

DUNDEE UNITED FC

Founded: 1909 (**Entered League**: 1910)
Former Names: Dundee Hibernians FC
Nickname: 'The Terrors'
Ground: Tannadice Park, Tannadice Street, Dundee, DD3 7JW
Ground Capacity: 14,223 (all seats)
Record Attendance: 28,000 (November 1966)
Pitch Size: 110 × 72 yards
Colours: Tangerine shirts with Black shorts
Telephone Nº: (01382) 833166
Ticket Office: (01382) 833166
Fax Number: (01382) 889398
Web Site: www.dundeeunitedfc.co.uk
E-mail: admin@dundeeunitedfc.co.uk

GENERAL INFORMATION

Car Parking: Street Parking only
Coach Parking: Gussie Park (home coaches)
Nearest Railway Station: Dundee (20 minutes walk)
Nearest Bus Station: Dundee
Club Shop: In Tannadice Street
Opening Times: Monday to Friday 9.00am to 5.00pm. Saturdays (away matches) 9.00am–1.00pm. Saturday/Sunday matchdays 9.00am to kick-off then 30 minutes after the game.
Telephone Nº: (01382) 833166

GROUND INFORMATION

Away Supporters' Entrances & Sections:
Turnstiles 7-16 for Jerry Kerr Stand & Jim McLean Fair Play Stand

ADMISSION INFO (2013/2014 PRICES)

Adult Seating: £19.00 – £27.00
Concessionary Seating: £10.00 – £15.00
Note: Prices vary depending on the category of the game
Programme Price: £3.00

DISABLED INFORMATION

Wheelchairs: Accommodated in the George Fox Stand, the Eddie Thompson Stand and Jim McLean Fair Play Stand.
Helpers: Please phone the club for details
Prices: Please phone the club for details
Disabled Toilets: Available in the George Fox Stand, the Eddie Thompson Stand and Jim McLean Fair Play Stand.
Contact: (01382) 833166 (Bookings are necessary)

Travelling Supporters' Information:
Routes: From the South or West: Travel via Perth and take the A90 to Dundee. Once in Dundee join the Kingsway (ring road) and follow until the third exit marked "Football Traffic", then turn right onto Old Glamis Road. Follow the road to join Provost Road then turn left into Sandeman Street for the ground; From the North: Follow the A90 from Aberdeen and join the Kingsway (ring road). At the first set of traffic lights turn right into Clepington Road and follow into Arklay Street before turning right into Tannadice Street for the ground.

HEART OF MIDLOTHIAN FC

Founded: 1874 (**Entered League**: 1890)
Nickname: 'The Jam Tarts' 'Jambos'
Ground: Tynecastle Stadium, Gorgie Road, Edinburgh EH11 2NL
Ground Capacity: 17,590 (All seats)
Record Attendance: 53,496 (13th January 1932)

Pitch Size: 109 × 70 yards (100 × 64 metres)
Colours: Maroon shirts and shorts
Telephone/Ticket Office N°: 0871 663-1874
Fax Number: (0131) 200-7222
Web Site: www.heartsfc.co.uk
E-mail: hearts@homplc.co.uk

GENERAL INFORMATION

Car Parking: Street Parking in Robertson Avenue and Wheatfield Road but none available at the ground itself
Coach Parking: Russell Road
Nearest Railway Station: Edinburgh Haymarket (½ mile)
Nearest Bus Station: St. Andrew's Square
Club Store: McLeod Street, Edinburgh
Opening Times: Weekdays 9.00am to 5.00pm, Saturday Matchdays 10.00am to 3.00pm, Non-match Saturdays 10.00am to 4.00pm and closed on Sundays.
Telephone N°: 0871 663-1874

GROUND INFORMATION

Away Supporters' Entrances & Sections:
Roseburn Stand entrances and accommodation

ADMISSION INFO (2013/2014 PRICES)

Adult Seating: £18.00 – £35.00
Senior Citizen Seating: £13.00 – £26.00
Under-18s Seating: £13.00 – £22.00
Under-12s Seating: £8.00 – £20.00
Note: Prices vary depending on the category of the game but very few seats will be available for most home games
Programme: £3.50

DISABLED INFORMATION

Wheelchairs: 100 spaces available for home and away fans in Wheatfield, Roseburn & Gorgie Stands
Helpers: Admitted
Prices: Please contact the club for further details
Disabled Toilets: Available
Contact: 0871 663-1874 Option 1 (Bookings are necessary)

Travelling Supporters' Information:
Routes: From the West: Take the A71 (Ayr Road) into Gorgie Road and the ground is about ¾ mile past Saughton Park on the left; From the North: Take the A90 Queensferry Road and turn right into Drum Brae after about ½ mile. Follow Drum Brae into Meadowplace Road (about 1 mile) then Broomhouse Road to the junction with Calder Road. Turn right, then as from the West; From the South: Take the A702/A703 to the A720 (Oxgangs Road). Turn left and follow the A720 into Wester Hailes Road (2½ miles) until the junction with Calder Road. Turn right, then as from the West.

HIBERNIAN FC

Founded: 1875 (**Entered League**: 1893)
Nickname: 'The Hi-Bees'
Ground: Easter Road Stadium, 12 Albion Place, Edinburgh EH7 5QG
Ground Capacity: 20,421 (all seats)
Record Attendance: 65,840 (2nd January 1950)
Pitch Size: 115 × 74 yards

Colours: Green and White shirts with White shorts
Telephone Nº: (0131) 661-2159
Ticket Office: (0131) 661-1875
Fax Number: (0131) 659-6488
Web Site: www.hibernianfc.co.uk
E-mail: club@hibernianfc.co.uk

GENERAL INFORMATION

Car Parking: Street parking
Coach Parking: Regent Road (by Police Direction)
Nearest Railway Station: Edinburgh Waverley (25 minutes walk)
Nearest Bus Station: St. Andrews Square
Club Shop: Famous Five Stand
Opening Times: Monday to Friday 9.00am – 5.00pm, Saturday Matchdays 9.00am – 3.00pm and ½ hour after the game. Non-matchday Saturdays 9.00am – 5.00pm
Club Shop e-mail: shopcounter@hibernianfc.co.uk
Telephone Nº: (0131) 656-7078

GROUND INFORMATION

Away Supporters' Entrances & Sections:
South Stand entrances and accommodation

ADMISSION INFO (2013/2014 PRICES)

Adult Seating: £22.00 – £30.00
Concessionary Seating: £12.00 – £17.00
Note: Prices vary depending on the category of the game.
Programme Price: £3.00

DISABLED INFORMATION

Wheelchairs: 14 spaces in the West Stand, 16 spaces in the East Stand, 11 spaces in the Famous Five Stand + 11 spaces in the South Stand. Also, 46 dual spaces in both the South Stand and Famous Five Stand
Helpers: One helper admitted per disabled person
Prices: Concessionary prices for the disabled and helpers
Disabled Toilets: 4 available in the Famous Five and South Stands, 5 in the West Stand and 2 in the East Stand
Contact: (0131) 656-7066
(Bookings are necessary for home supporters. Away Supporters should book and pay through their own club)

Travelling Supporters' Information:
Routes: From the West and North: Take the A90 Queensferry Road to the A902 and continue for 2¼ miles. Turn right into Great Junction Street and follow into Duke Street then Lochend Road. Turn sharp right into Hawkhill Avenue at Lochend Park and follow the road into Albion Place for the ground; From the South: Take the A1 through Musselburgh (Milton Road/Willow Brae/London Road) and turn right into Easter Road after about 2½ miles. Take the 4th right into Albion Road for the ground.

INVERNESS CALEDONIAN THISTLE FC

Founded: 1994 (**Entered League**: 1994)
Former Names: Caledonian Thistle FC
Nickname: 'The Jags' 'Caley'
Ground: Tulloch Caledonian Stadium, Stadium Road, Inverness IV1 1FF
Ground Capacity: 7,700 (all seats)
Record Attendance: 7,700

Colours: Shirts are Royal Blue and Red, Shorts are Royal Blue
Telephone Nº: (01463) 222880 (Ground)
Ticket Office: (01463) 222880
Fax Number: (01463) 227479
Web Site: www.ictfc.co.uk

GENERAL INFORMATION

Car Parking: At the ground
Coach Parking: At the ground
Nearest Railway Station: Inverness (1 mile)
Nearest Bus Station: Inverness
Club Shop: At the ground
Opening Times: Weekdays and Matchdays 9.00am–4.30pm
Telephone Nº: (01463) 222880

GROUND INFORMATION

Away Supporters' Entrances & Sections:
South Stand

ADMISSION INFO (2013/2014 PRICES)

Adult Seating: £16.00 – £30.00
Child Seating: £7.00 – £25.00
Senior Citizen Seating: £16.00 – £26.00
Note: Prices vary depending on the category of the game.
Programme Price: £2.50

DISABLED INFORMATION

Wheelchairs: 52 spaces available in total
Helpers: Admitted
Prices: Free of charge for the disabled and their helpers
Disabled Toilets: Available
Contact: (01463) 222880 (Bookings are necessary)

Travelling Supporters' Information:
Routes: The ground is adjacent to Kessock Bridge. From the South: Take the A9 to Inverness and turn right at the roundabout before the bridge over the Moray Firth; From the North: Take the A9 over the bridge and turn left at the roundabout for the ground.

KILMARNOCK FC

Founded: 1869 (**Entered League**: 1896)
Nickname: 'Killie'
Ground: Rugby Park, Rugby Road, Kilmarnock, Ayrshire KA1 2DP
Record Attendance: 34,246 (17th August 1963)
Pitch Size: 115 × 74 yards
Ground Capacity: 18,128 (all seats)

Colours: Shirts are Blue with broad White stripes, White shorts
Telephone N°: (01563) 545300
Fax Number: (01563) 522181
Ticket Office N°: (01563) 545318
Web Site: www.kilmarnockfc.co.uk

GENERAL INFORMATION

Car Parking: At the ground (Permit Holders only)
Coach Parking: Fairyhill Road Bus Park
Nearest Railway Station: Kilmarnock (15 minutes walk)
Nearest Bus Station: Kilmarnock (10 minutes walk)
Club Shop: Adjacent to the West Stand at the ground
Opening Times: Monday to Friday 9.00am – 5.00pm, Saturdays 10.00am – 2.00pm (until kick-off on matchdays)
Telephone N°: (01563) 545310

GROUND INFORMATION

Away Supporters' Entrances & Sections:
Rugby Road turnstiles for the Chadwick Stand

ADMISSION INFO (2013/2014 PRICES)

Adult Seating: £22.00 – £26.00
Concessionary Seating: £10.00 – £15.00
Under-12s Seating: £5.00 (if accompanied by an adult)
Note: Prices for games against Rangers & Celtic are £26.00 with only 200 concessionary tickets available at £17.00. These tickets are allocated on a first-come first-served basis
Programme Price: £2.50

DISABLED INFORMATION

Wheelchairs: 15 spaces each for home and away fans in the Main Stand
Helpers: One helper admitted per wheelchair
Prices: Prices vary depending on reciprocal arrangements
Disabled Toilets: 2 available in the Chadwick Stand and Moffat Stand
Contact: Kilmarnock FC Disabled Supporters' Association on (01563) 545300

Travelling Supporters' Information:
Routes: From Glasgow/Ayr: Take the A77 Kilmarnock Bypass. Exit at the Bellfield Interchange. Take the A71 (Irvine) to the first roundabout then take the A759 (Kilmarnock Town Centre). The ground is ½ mile on the left hand side.

MOTHERWELL FC

Founded: 1886 (**Entered League**: 1893)
Nickname: 'The Steelmen'
Ground: Firpark, Firpark Street, Motherwell, ML1 2QN
Ground Capacity: 13,664 (all seats)
Record Attendance: 35,632 (12th March 1952)
Pitch Size: 102 × 68 yards

Colours: Shirts are Amber with a Claret chestband and Claret trim, Shorts are Amber with Claret trim
Telephone/Ticket Office N°: (01698) 333333
Fax Number: (01698) 338001
Web Site: www.motherwellfc.co.uk
E-mail: mfcenquiries@motherwellfc.co.uk

GENERAL INFORMATION

Car Parking: Street parking and nearby Car Parks
Coach Parking: Orbiston Street
Nearest Railway Station: Airbles (1 mile)
Nearest Bus Station: Motherwell
Club Shop: At the ground
Opening Times: Weekdays 9.30am to 4.00pm plus Saturday Matchdays from 9.30am to 5.30pm
Telephone N°: (01698) 338025

GROUND INFORMATION

Away Supporters' Entrances & Sections:
Dalziel Drive entrances for the South Stand

ADMISSION INFO (2013/2014 PRICES)

Adult Seating: £18.00 – £25.00
Under-16s Seating: £9.00 – £14.00
Concessionary Seating: £15.00 – £17.00
Note: Discounts are available in the Family Section and prices vary depending on the category of the game
Programme Price: £2.50

DISABLED INFORMATION

Wheelchairs: 20 spaces for home fans and 10 spaces for away fans in the South-West enclosure.
Helpers: Admitted
Prices: Please phone the club for information
Disabled Toilets: One available close to the Disabled Area
Contact: (01698) 338009 (Must book 1 week in advance)

Travelling Supporters' Information:
Routes: From the East: Take the A723 into Merry Street and turn left into Brandon Street (1 mile). Follow through to Windmill Hill Street and turn right at the Fire Station into Knowetop Avenue for the ground; From Elsewhere: Exit the M74 at Junction 4 and take the A723 Hamilton Road into the Town Centre. Turn right into West Hamilton Street and follow into Brandon Street – then as from the East.

PARTICK THISTLE FC

Founded: 1876 (**Entered League**: 1890)
Nickname: 'The Jags'
Ground: Firhill Stadium, 80 Firhill Road, Glasgow, G20 7AL
Ground Capacity: 10,921 (All seats)
Record Attendance: 49,838 (18th February 1922)
Pitch Size: 115 × 75 yards

Colours: Red and Yellow striped shirts, Red shorts
Telephone Nº: 0871 402-1971
Ticket Office: 0871 402-1971
Fax Number: (0141) 945-1525
Web Site: www.ptfc.co.uk
e-mail: mail@ptfc.co.uk

GENERAL INFORMATION

Car Parking: Street parking
Coach Parking: Panmure Street
Nearest Railway Station: Maryhill
Nearest Underground Station: St. George's Cross
Club Shops: Greaves Sports – www.greavessports.com
Opening Times: Matchdays 12.00pm to 5.00pm or 5.30pm to 9.30pm for Night matches.
Telephone Nº: 0871 402-1971

GROUND INFORMATION

Away Supporters' Entrances & Sections:
North Stand (enter via Firhill Road turnstiles)

ADMISSION INFO (2013/2014 PRICES)

Please contact the club directly for details of ticket prices and availability during the 2013/2014 season.

DISABLED INFORMATION

Wheelchairs: 17 spaces in the North Enclosure
Helpers: One helper admitted per wheelchair
Prices: Free for the disabled and one helper
Disabled Toilets: Available in the North Enclosure and the North Stand
Contact: 0871 402-1971 (Bookings are necessary)

Travelling Supporters' Information:
Routes: From the East: Exit the M8 at Junction 16; From the West: Exit the M8 at Junction 17. From both directions, follow Maryhill Road to Queen's Cross and the ground is on the right.

ROSS COUNTY FC

Founded: 1929 (**Entered League**: 1994)
Nickname: 'The Staggies'
Ground: GLobal Energy Stadium, Victoria Park, Dingwall, Ross-shire, IV15 9QW
Ground Capacity: 6,500
Seating Capacity: 6,500
Record Attendance: 10,000 (19th February 1966)

Pitch Size: 115 × 74 yards
Colours: Navy Blue shirts and shorts
Telephone Nº: (01349) 860860
Ticket Office: (01349) 860860
Fax Number: (01349) 866277
Web Site: www.rosscountyfootballclub.co.uk
E-mail: info@rosscountyfootballclub.co.uk

GENERAL INFORMATION

Car Parking: At the ground
Coach Parking: At the ground
Nearest Railway Station: Dingwall (adjacent)
Nearest Bus Station: Dingwall
Club Shop: At the ground
Opening Times: Weekdays and Matchdays
Telephone Nº: (01349) 860860

GROUND INFORMATION

Away Supporters' Entrances & Sections:
North Stand entrances and accommodation

ADMISSION INFO (2013/2014 PRICES)

Adult Seating: £20.00 – £26.00
Under-16s Seating: £10.00 – £12.00
Concessionary Seating: £12.00 – £16.00
Note: Prices vary depending on the category of the game
Programme Price: £2.00

DISABLED INFORMATION

Wheelchairs: 6 spaces each for home and away fans
Helpers: Admitted
Prices: Normal prices are charged
Disabled Toilets: Available at the bottom of the West Stand
Contact: (01349) 860860 (Bookings are necessary)

Travelling Supporters' Information:
Routes: The ground is situated at Dingwall adjacent to the Railway Station which is down Jubilee Park Road at the bottom of the High Street.

ST. JOHNSTONE FC

Founded: 1884 (**Entered League**: 1911)
Nickname: 'Saints'
Ground: McDiarmid Park, Crieff Road, Perth, PH1 2SJ
Ground Capacity: 10,740 (All seats)
Record Attendance: 10,545 (23rd May 1999)
Pitch Size: 115 × 75 yards

Colours: Blue shirts with White shorts
Telephone Nº: (01738) 459090
Ticket Office: (01738) 455000
Fax Number: (01738) 625771
Web Site: www.perthstjohnstonefc.co.uk

GENERAL INFORMATION

Car Parking: Car park at the ground
Coach Parking: At the ground
Nearest Railway Station: Perth (3 miles)
Nearest Bus Station: Perth (3 miles)
Club Shop: At the ground
Opening Times: Weekdays from 9.00am to 5.00pm and Matchdays 1.30pm to 3.00pm
Telephone Nº: (01738) 459090

GROUND INFORMATION

Away Supporters' Entrances & Sections:
North Stand and North End of the West Stand and South Stand

ADMISSION INFO (2013/2014 PRICES)

Adult Seating: £22.00 – £23.00
Under-18s Seating: £8.00 (East Stand only)
Under-16s Seating: £8.00 – £13.00
Senior Citizens: £12.00 – £14.00
Programme Price: £2.50

DISABLED INFORMATION

Wheelchairs: 8 spaces available for home fans in both the East and West Stands. 8 spaces for away fans in the West Stand.
Helpers: Please phone the club for details
Prices: Please phone the club for details
Disabled Toilets: Available in the East and West Stands
Contact: (01738) 459090 (Bookings are necessary)

Travelling Supporters' Information:
Routes: Follow the M80 to Stirling, take the A9 Inverness Road north from Perth and follow the signs for the 'Football Stadium'. The ground is situated beside a dual-carriageway – the Perth Western By-pass near Junction 11 of the M90.

ST. MIRREN FC

Founded: 1877 (**Entered League**: 1890)
Nickname: 'The Saints' 'The Buddies'
Ground: St. Mirren Park, Greenhill Road, Paisley, PA3 1RU
Ground Capacity: 8,023 (all seats)
Record Attendance: 47,428 (7th March 1925 – at former stadium in Love Street)

Pitch Size: 115 × 74 yards
Colours: Black and White striped shirts, Black shorts
Telephone N°: (0141) 889-2558
Ticket Line N°: (0141) 840-4100
Fax Number: (0141) 848-6444
Web Site: www.saintmirren.net
E-mail: info@saintmirren.net

GENERAL INFORMATION

Car Parking: Street parking
Coach Parking: Clark Street
Nearest Railway Station: Paisley St. James (400 yards) or Paisley Gilmour Street (10 minutes walk)
Nearest Bus Station: Paisley
Club Shop: At the stadium
Opening Times: Daily from 9.00am to 5.00pm
Telephone N°: (0141) 840-4100

GROUND INFORMATION

Away Supporters' Entrances & Sections:
North Stand (N1-N5), turnstiles 17-20

ADMISSION INFO (2013/2014 PRICES)

Adult Seating: £20.00 – £22.00
Concessionary Seating: £10.00 – £12.00
Under-18s Seating: £10.00 – £12.00
Under-12s Seating: £5.00 – £12.00
Note: Under-12s pay £2.00 in the Family Stand
Programme Price: £2.50

DISABLED INFORMATION

Wheelchairs: Accommodated in all Stands
Helpers: Admitted
Prices: Disabled fans and helpers each pay £10.00.
Disabled Toilets: Available in all the stands
Contact: (0141) 840-4100 (Bookings are necessary)

Travelling Supporters' Information:
Routes: From All Parts: Exit the M8 at Junction 29 and take the A726, keeping in the middle lane to avoid the A727 which is signposted for Irvine. At the St. James interchange, turn left onto the dual carriageway (Greenock Road) which has football pitches on the left. After the sharp bend, take the first turn on the right into Clark Street and, at the T-junction, turn left past the railway station into Greenhill Road. The stadium is on the right-hand side of the road.

The Scottish Professional Football League – Division One

Address

National Stadium, Hampden Park,
Mount Florida, Glasgow G42 9DE

Phone (0141) 620-4140

Fax (0141) 620-4141

Clubs for the 2013/2014 Season

ALLOA ATHLETIC FC

Founded: 1878 (**Entered League**: 1921)
Nickname: 'The Wasps'
Ground: Recreation Park, Clackmannan Road, Alloa, FK10 1RY
Ground Capacity: 3,100
Seating Capacity: 900
Record Attendance: 13,000 (26th February 1939)

Pitch Size: 110 × 75 yards
Colours: Gold and Black shirts with Black shorts
Telephone Nº: (01259) 722695
Ticket Office: (01259) 722695
Fax Number: (01259) 210886
Web Site: www.alloaathletic.co.uk
E-mail: fcadmin@alloaathletic.co.uk

GENERAL INFORMATION

Car Parking: A Car Park is adjacent to the ground
Coach Parking: By Police Direction
Nearest Railway Station: Alloa
Nearest Bus Station: Alloa
Club Shop: At the ground
Opening Times: Matchdays only 1.30pm to 5.00pm
Telephone Nº: (01259) 722695

GROUND INFORMATION

Away Supporters' Entrances & Sections:
Hilton Road entrance for the Hilton Road Side and Clackmannan Road End

ADMISSION INFO (2013/2014 PRICES)

Adult Standing: £14.00
Adult Seating: £14.00
Senior Citizen/Child Standing: £7.00
Senior Citizen/Child Seating: £7.00
Programme Price: £2.00

DISABLED INFORMATION

Wheelchairs: Accommodated in the Disabled Section underneath the Main Stand
Helpers: Admitted
Prices: Free of charge for the disabled and helpers
Disabled Toilets: One available in the Main Stand
Contact: (01259) 722695 (Bookings are not necessary)

Travelling Supporters' Information:
Routes: From the South and East: Take the M74 to the M80 and exit at Junction 9 following the A907 into Alloa. Continue over two roundabouts passing the brewery and Town Centre. The Ground is on the left-hand side of the road.

COWDENBEATH FC

Founded: 1881 (**Entered League**: 1905)
Nickname: 'Cowden' 'Blue Brazil'
Ground: Central Park, High Street, Cowdenbeath KY4 9QQ
Ground Capacity: 4,370 **Seating Capacity**: 1,431
Record Attendance: 25,586 (21st September 1949)
Pitch Size: 107 × 64 yards

Colours: Shirts are Royal Blue with White trim, Shorts are White
Telephone Nº: (01383) 610166
Ticket Office: (01383) 610166
Fax Number: (01383) 512132
Web Site: www.cowdenbeathfc.com
E-mail: office@cowdenbeathfc.com

GENERAL INFORMATION

Car Parking: Car Park at the ground and Stenhouse Street (200 yards). A total of 200 spaces are available
Coach Parking: King Street and Rowan Terrace
Nearest Railway Station: Cowdenbeath (400 yards)
Nearest Bus Station: Cowdenbeath (Bus Stop at ground)
Club Shop: At the ground
Opening Times: Weekdays 9.00am to 5.00pm and Matchdays 10.00am to 5.00pm
Telephone Nº: (01383) 610166

GROUND INFORMATION

Away Supporters' Entrances & Sections:
High Street end of the ground

ADMISSION INFO (2013/2014 PRICES)

Adult Standing: £15.00
Adult Seating: £15.00
Child Standing/Seating: £8.00 (Ages 16 and under)
Senior Citizen Standing/Seating: £8.00
Family Ticket: £16.00 (1 adult + 1 child aged 12 or under)
Programme Price: £2.00

DISABLED INFORMATION

Wheelchairs: 3 spaces each for home and away fans
Helpers: Please phone the club for information
Prices: Free for disabled fans but helpers pay normal prices
Disabled Toilets: 1 Ladies, 1 Gents and 1 Unisex available
Contact: (01383) 610166 (Bookings are necessary)

Travelling Supporters' Information:
Routes: Exit the M90 at Junction 3 for Dunfermline. Take the Dual Carriageway to Cowdenbeath and follow straight on into the High Street. The ground is situated on the first left turn in the High Street.

DUMBARTON FC

Founded: 1872 (**Entered League**: 1890)
Nickname: 'Sons'
Ground: Dumbarton Football Stadium, Castle Road, Dumbarton G82 1JJ
Ground Capacity: 2,046 (All seats)
Record Attendance: 2,035 (27th January 2001)
Pitch Size: 110 × 72 yards

Colours: Gold shirts and shorts
Telephone N°: (01389) 762569
Ticket Office: (01389) 762569
Fax Number: (01389) 762629
Web Site: www.dumbartonfootballclub.com
E-mail: enquiries@dumbartonfc.com

GENERAL INFORMATION

Car Parking: 400 spaces available at the ground
Coach Parking: At the ground
Nearest Railway Station: Dumbarton East
Nearest Bus Station: Dumbarton
Club Shop: At the ground
Opening Times: Monday, Wednesday, Friday and Saturday matchdays 9.30am to 3.30pm
Telephone N°: (01389) 762569

GROUND INFORMATION

Away Supporters' Entrances & Sections:
West Section

ADMISSION INFO (2013/2014 PRICES)

Adult Seating: £15.00
Child Seating: £8.00
Family Ticket: £20.00 (1 adult + 1 child)
Programme Price: £2.00

DISABLED INFORMATION

Wheelchairs: Approximately 24 spaces available in the disabled area
Helpers: Please phone the club for information
Prices: Please phone the club for information
Disabled Toilets: Available
Contact: (01389) 762569 (Bookings are necessary)

Travelling Supporters' Information:
Routes: The ground is situated just by Dumbarton Castle. Take the A814 into Dumbarton and follow the brown signs for the Castle to find the ground.

DUNDEE FC

Founded: 1893 (**Entered League**: 1893)
Nickname: 'The Dee'
Ground: Dens Park Stadium, Sandeman Street, Dundee DD3 7JY
Ground Capacity: 11,850 (All seats)
Record Attendance: 43,024 (7th February 1953)

Pitch Size: 105 × 70 yards
Colours: Blue shirts with White shorts
Telephone Nº: (01382) 889966
Ticket Office: (01382) 889966
Fax Number: (01382) 832284
Web Site: www.dundeefc.co.uk

GENERAL INFORMATION

Car Parking: Street parking only
Coach Parking: Please contact the club for details
Nearest Railway Station: Dundee
Nearest Bus Station: Dundee
Club Shop: At the Stadium
Opening Times: Weekdays from 10.00am to 5.00pm
Telephone Nº: (01382) 889966

GROUND INFORMATION

Away Supporters' Entrances & Sections:
Turnstiles 33-38 for East Stand accommodation

ADMISSION INFO (2013/2014 PRICES)

Adult Seating: £19.00
Child Seating: £10.00
Senior Citizen Seating: £10.00
Programme Price: £2.50

DISABLED INFORMATION

Wheelchairs: Accommodated in the East and West Stands
Helpers: Admitted free of charge
Prices: £10.00 for the disabled in the Disabled Area only
Disabled Toilets: Adjacent to the Disabled Area
Contact: (01382) 889966 (Bookings are necessary)

Travelling Supporters' Information:
Routes: Take the A972 from Perth (Kingsway West) to King's Cross Circus Roundabout. Take the 3rd exit into Clepington Road and turn right into Provost Road for 1 mile then take the 2nd left into Sandeman Street for the ground.

FALKIRK FC

Founded: 1876 (**Entered League**: 1902)
Nickname: 'The Bairns'
Ground: The Falkirk Stadium, 6 Stadium Way, Falkirk FK2 9EE
Ground Capacity: 8,003 (All seats)
Pitch Size: 112 x 75 yards

Colours: Navy Blue shirts with White shorts
Telephone Nº: (01324) 624121
Ticket Office: (01324) 624121
Web Site: www.falkirkfc.co.uk
E-mail: post@falkirkfc.co.uk

GENERAL INFORMATION

Car Parking: A large Car Park is adjacent
Coach Parking: Available nearby
Nearest Railway Station: Falkirk Grahamston (1 mile)
Nearest Bus Station: Falkirk (1 mile)
Club Shop: At the stadium
Opening Times: 10.00am to 4.00pm
Telephone Nº: (01324) 624121

GROUND INFORMATION

Away Supporters' Entrances & Sections:
North Stand

ADMISSION INFO (2013/2014 PRICES)

Adult Seating: £18.00 – £23.00
Under-18s Seating: £6.00 – £7.00 (Under-5s admitted free)
Concessionary Seating: £12.00 – £13.00
Programme Price: £2.50 (Price may change this season)

DISABLED INFORMATION

Wheelchairs: Accommodated
Helpers: Admitted
Prices: Free of charge for the disabled and helpers
Disabled Toilets: Available
Contact: (01324) 624121 (Bookings are necessary)

Travelling Supporters' Information:
Routes: Exit the M9 at Junction 6 and take the A904 towards Falkirk. Continue into Falkirk at the Westfield/Laurieston roundabout along Grangemouth Road and take the first right into Alexander Avenue. Then take the 2nd right into Westfield Street and the ground is on the right.

GREENOCK MORTON FC

Founded: 1874 (**Entered League**: 1893)
Nickname: 'Ton'
Ground: Cappielow Park, Sinclair Street, Greenock, PA15 2TY
Ground Capacity: 11,589 **Seating Capacity**: 6,039
Record Attendance: 23,500 (29th April 1921)

Pitch Size: 110 × 71 yards
Colours: Blue and White hooped shirts, Blue shorts
Telephone/Ticket Office Nº: (01475) 723571
Fax Number: (01475) 781084
Web Site: www.gmfc.net
E-mail: admin@gmfc.net

GENERAL INFORMATION

Car Parking: At the ground (£3.00 fee) or Street parking
Coach Parking: James Watt Dock
Nearest Railway Station: Cartsdyke (½ mile)
Nearest Bus Station: Town Centre (1½ miles)
Club Shop: Within "Smiths of Greenock", West Blackhall Street, Greenock. There is also a Merchandise Unit in Sinclair Street, outside of the ground open matchdays only.
Opening Times: Monday to Saturday 9.00am to 5.00pm
Telephone Nº: (01475) 888555 **Fax Nº**: (01475) 781084
Club Shop Web Site: www.themortonshop.com

GROUND INFORMATION

Away Supporters' Entrances & Sections:
East Hamilton Street turnstiles

ADMISSION INFO (2013/2014 PRICES)

Adult Standing and Seating: £15.00
Under-16s Standing: £5.00 (Under-12s £3.00 with a paying adult; Under-5s admitted free with a paying adult)
Parent and Child Seating: £18.00
Senior Citizen Standing and Seating: £10.00
Concessionary Standing and Seating: £10.00
Programme Price: £2.50

DISABLED INFORMATION

Wheelchairs: 5 spaces each for home and away fans accommodated below the Grandstand
Helpers: One helper admitted per disabled fan
Prices: £10.00 for the disabled, free of charge for helpers
Disabled Toilets: One available
Contact: (01475) 723571 (Bookings are necessary)

Travelling Supporters' Information:
Routes: From the North: Take the M8 to the A8. From Port Glasgow follow the A78 to Greenock. Cappielow Park is on the left after passing under the railway bridge; From the South: Take the A78 to Greenock. Follow the road past IBM then turn right at the second set of lights into Dunlop Street. Follow this road until it turns sharp left and goes downhill and continue to the traffic lights facing the river. Turn right onto the A8, cross two roundabouts and Capplielow Park is on the right hand side of the road.

HAMILTON ACADEMICAL FC

Founded: 1874 (**Entered League**: 1897)
Nickname: 'The Accies'
Ground: New Douglas Park, Hamilton ML3 0FT
Ground Capacity: 6,078 (all seats)
Record Attendance: 5,895 (25th February 2009)
Pitch Size: 115 × 75 yards

Colours: Red and White hooped shirts, shorts are White with a Red flash
Telephone Nº: (01698) 368652
Fax Number: (01698) 285422
Web Site: www.acciesfc.co.uk
E-mail: scott@acciesfc.co.uk

GENERAL INFORMATION

Car Parking: In the adjacent Caird Street Council Car Park
Coach Parking: In the Caird Street Car Park
Nearest Railway Station: Hamilton West (200 yards)
Nearest Bus Station: Hamilton (1 mile)
Club Shop: At the stadium
Opening Times: Monday, Tuesday, Thursday and Friday 9.30am to 4.30pm.
Telephone Nº: (01698) 368658

GROUND INFORMATION

Away Supporters' Entrances & Sections:
North and East Stands – use turnstiles 7 to 12

ADMISSION INFO (2013/2014 PRICES)

Adult Seating: £16.00
Under-18s Seating: £8.00
Senior Citizen Seating: £8.00
Programme Price: £2.50

DISABLED INFORMATION

Wheelchairs: Accommodated in the front row of the stand or by the trackside
Helpers: Admitted following prior booking
Prices: £10.00 in total for each disabled fan and helper
Disabled Toilets: Available
Contact: (01698) 368652 (Bookings are necessary)

Travelling Supporters' Information:
Routes: Exit the M74 at Junction 5 and follow signs marked "Football Traffic". Go past Hamilton Racecourse, turn right at the lights by Hamilton Business Park then first right again for New Park Street and Auchinraith Avenue. The ground is behind Morrisons and Sainsburys.

LIVINGSTON FC

Founded: 1943 (**Entered League**: 1974)
Former Names: Ferranti Thistle FC, Meadowbank Thistle FC
Nickname: 'The Lions'
Ground: Almondvale Stadium, Alderstone Road, Livingston EH54 7DN
Ground Capacity: 10,006 (All seats)

Record Attendance: 10,006 (vs Rangers)
Pitch Size: 105 × 72 yards
Colours: Gold shirts with Black shorts
Telephone Nº: (01506) 417000
Fax Number: (01506) 429948
Web Site: www.livingstonfc.co.uk
E-mail: lfcreception@livingstonfc.co.uk

GENERAL INFORMATION

Car Parking: Car Park at the ground by arrangement
Coach Parking: At the ground
Nearest Railway Station: Livingston
Nearest Bus Station: Livingston
Club Shop: At the Stadium
Opening Times: Daily – please phone for further details

GROUND INFORMATION

Away Supporters' Entrances & Sections:
East Stand entrances and accommodation

ADMISSION INFO (2013/2014 PRICES)

Adult Seating: £16.00
Concessionary Seating: £10.00
Under-16s Seating: £5.00
Programme Price: £2.00

DISABLED INFORMATION

Wheelchairs: Accommodated
Helpers: Please phone the club for information
Prices: Please phone the club for information
Disabled Toilets: Available
Contact: (01506) 417000 (Bookings are necessary)

Travelling Supporters' Information:
Routes: Exit the M8 at the Livingston turn-off and take the A899 to the Cousland Interchange. Turn right into Cousland Road, pass the Hospital, then turn left into Alderstone Road and the stadium is on the left opposite the Campus.

QUEEN OF THE SOUTH FC

Founded: 1919 (**Entered League**: 1923)
Nickname: 'The Doonhamers'
Ground: Palmerston Park, Terregles Street, Dumfries, DG2 9BA
Ground Capacity: 6,412
Seating Capacity: 3,509
Record Attendance: 26,552 (23rd February 1952)

Pitch Size: 112 × 73 yards
Colours: Blue shirts with White shorts
Telephone N°: (01387) 254853
Ticket Office: (01387) 254853
Fax Number: (01387) 240470
Web Site: www.qosfc.com
E-mail: admin@qosfc.com

GENERAL INFORMATION

Car Parking: Car Park adjacent to the ground
Coach Parking: Car Park adjacent to the ground
Nearest Railway Station: Dumfries (¾ mile)
Nearest Bus Station: Dumfries Whitesands (5 minutes walk)
Club Shop: At the ground
Opening Times: Daily
Telephone N°: (01387) 254853

GROUND INFORMATION

Away Supporters' Entrances & Sections:
Terregles Street entrances for the East Stand

ADMISSION INFO (2013/2014 PRICES)

Adult Standing: £16.00
Adult Seating: £16.00
Senior Citizen Standing/Seating: £9.00
Under-16s Standing/Seating: £5.00
Programme Price: £2.50

DISABLED INFORMATION

Wheelchairs: Accommodated in front of the East Stand
Helpers: Admitted
Prices: Free of charge for disabled fans and helpers
Disabled Toilets: One available in the East Stand
Contact: (01387) 254853 (Bookings are necessary)

Travelling Supporters' Information:
Routes: From the East: Take the A75 to Dumfries and follow the ring road over the River Nith. Turn left at the 1st roundabout then right at the 2nd roundabout (the Kilmarnock/Glasgow Road roundabout). The ground is a short way along past the Tesco store; From the West: Take the A75 to Dumfries and proceed along ring road to the 1st roundabout (Kilmarnock/Glasgow Road) then as from the East; From the North: Take A76 to Dumfries and carry straight across 1st roundabout for the ground.

RAITH ROVERS FC

Founded: 1883 (**Entered League**: 1902)
Nickname: 'The Rovers'
Ground: Stark's Park, Pratt Street, Kirkcaldy, KY1 1SA
Ground Capacity: 10,104 (All seats)
Record Attendance: 31,306 (7th February 1953)
Pitch Size: 113 × 70 yards

Colours: Navy Blue shirts with White shorts
Telephone Nº: (01592) 263514
Ticket Office: (01592) 263514
Fax Number: (01592) 642833
Web Site: www.raithrovers.net
E-mail: football@raithrovers.net

GENERAL INFORMATION

Car Parking: Esplanade and Beveridge Car Park
Coach Parking: Railway Station & Esplanade
Nearest Railway Station: Kirkcaldy (15 minutes walk)
Nearest Bus Station: Kirkcaldy (15 minutes walk)
Club Shop: ACA Sports, High Street, Kirkcaldy
Opening Times: Monday to Saturday 9.00am to 5.00pm
Telephone Nº: (01592) 263514

GROUND INFORMATION

Away Supporters' Entrances & Sections:
North Stand

ADMISSION INFO (2013/2014 PRICES)

Adult Seating: £17.00
Senior Citizen/Child Seating: £9.00
Note: One adult and one child are admitted for £20.00
Programme Price: £2.00

DISABLED INFORMATION

Wheelchairs: 12 spaces each for home and away fans accommodated in the North & South Stands
Helpers: One helper admitted per wheelchair
Prices: Free of charge for the helpers. Disabled pay concessionary prices
Disabled Toilets: Available in the North and South Stands
Are Bookings Necessary: Only for all-ticket games
Contact: (01592) 263514

Travelling Supporters' Information:
Routes: Take the M8 to the end then follow the A90/M90 over the Forth Road Bridge. Exit the M90 at Junction 1 and follow the A921 to Kirkcaldy. On the outskirts of town, turn left at the B & Q roundabout from which the floodlights can be seen. The ground is raised on the hill nearby.

The Scottish Professional Football League – Division Two

Address
National Stadium, Hampden Park,
Mount Florida, Glasgow G42 9DE

Phone (0141) 620-4140
Fax (0141) 620-4141

Clubs for the 2013/2014 Season

AIRDRIEONIANS FC

Founded: 1965 (**Entered League**: 1966)
Former Name: Clydebank FC and Airdrie United FC
Ground: Excelsior Stadium, Broomfield Park, Craigneuk Avenue, Airdrie ML6 8QZ
Ground Capacity: 10,170 (All seats)
Record Attendance: 9,612

Pitch Size: 115 × 71 yards
Colours: White shirts with Red diamond, White shorts
Telephone Nº: 07710 230775
Ticket Office: 07710 230775
Fax Number: (0141) 221-1497
Web Site: www.airdriefc.com

GENERAL INFORMATION

Car Parking: Behind all the Stands
Coach Parking: Behind the East Stand
Nearest Railway Station: Drumgelloch (½ mile)
Nearest Bus Station: Gartlea – Airdrie Town Centre
Club Shop: At the ground
Opening Times: Opens at 12.00pm on Home Matchdays and Sunday 2.00pm – 4.00pm
Telephone Nº: 07710 230775

GROUND INFORMATION

Away Supporters' Entrances & Sections:
East and South Stands

ADMISSION INFO (2013/2014 PRICES)

Adult Seating: £16.00
Under-16s Seating: £7.00
Senior Citizen Seating: £10.00
Note: Parent and Child tickets are priced at £20.00
Programme Price: £2.00

DISABLED INFORMATION

Wheelchairs: Spaces available for home and away fans accommodated in the front sections
Helpers: One admitted per disabled supporter
Prices: Each disabled supporter with a helper are admitted for half-price
Disabled Toilets: Available in all the stands
Contact: (07710) 230775 (Bookings are preferable)

Travelling Supporters' Information:
Routes: From the East: Exit the M8 at Junction 6 and take the A73 (signposted for Cumbernauld). Pass through Chapelhall into Airdrie and turn right into Petersburn Road – the ground is on the left; From the West: Take the A8 to the Chapelhall turn-off for Chapelhall. Join the A73 at Chapelhall, then as above.

ARBROATH FC

Founded: 1878 (**Entered League**: 1902)
Nickname: 'The Red Lichties'
Ground: Gayfield Park, Arbroath DD11 1QB
Ground Capacity: 5,940
Seating Capacity: 814
Record Attendance: 13,510 (23rd February 1952)

Pitch Size: 115 × 71 yards
Colours: Maroon and White shirts with Maroon shorts
Telephone Nº: (01241) 872157
Ticket Office: (01241) 872157
Fax Number: (01241) 431125
Web Site: www.arbroathfc.co.uk

GENERAL INFORMATION

Car Parking: Car Park in Queen's Drive
Coach Parking: Car Park in Queen's Drive
Nearest Railway Station: Arbroath (15 minutes walk)
Nearest Bus Station: Arbroath (10 minutes walk)
Club Shop: At the ground
Opening Times: Matchdays only 2.00pm – 5.00pm
Telephone Nº: (01241) 872157

GROUND INFORMATION

Away Supporters' Entrances & Sections:
Queen's Drive End

ADMISSION INFO (2013/2014 PRICES)

Adult Standing: £12.00
Adult Seating: £12.00
Concessionary Standing: £6.00
Concessionary Seating: £6.00
Family Ticket: 1 adult + 1 child £15.00
Programme Price: £2.00

DISABLED INFORMATION

Wheelchairs: 6 spaces available at both of the West and East Ends of the Main Stand
Helpers: Admitted
Prices: Normal prices for the disabled and helpers
Disabled Toilets: Two available at the rear of the Stand
Contact: (01241) 872157 (Bookings are not necessary)

Travelling Supporters' Information:
Routes: From Dundee and the West: Take the A92 (Coast Road). On entering Arbroath, pass under the Railway Line and the ground is on the right-hand side; From Stonehaven/Montrose: Take the A92, pass through Arbroath, go past the Harbour and the ground is on the left-hand side.

AYR UNITED FC

Founded: 1910 (**Entered League**: 1910)
Former Names: Formed by the amagamation of Ayr Parkhouse FC and Ayr FC in 1910
Nickname: 'The Honest Men'
Ground: Somerset Park, Tryfield Place, Ayr, KA8 9NB
Ground Capacity: 10,185
Seating Capacity: 1,500
Record Attendance: 25,225 (13th September 1969)
Pitch Size: 110 × 72 yards
Colours: White shirts with Black shorts
Telephone/Ticket Office Nº: (01292) 263435
Fax Number: (01292) 281314
Web site: www.ayrunitedfc.co.uk
E-mail: info@ayrunitedfc.co.uk

GENERAL INFORMATION

Car Parking: Craigie Car Park, Ayr Racecourse and Somerset Road Car Park
Coach Parking: Craigie Car Park
Nearest Railway Station: Ayr or Newton-on-Ayr (both stations are 10 minutes walk)
Nearest Bus Station: Sandgate, Ayr
Club Shop: At the ground
Opening Times: Monday to Friday 12.00pm to 4.00pm and Matchdays from 12.00pm to kick-off
Telephone Nº: (01292) 263435

GROUND INFORMATION

Away Supporters' Entrances & Sections:
Turnstiles 1-7 for the Railway End (covered terrace) + turnstiles 9-10 for Main Stand accommodation

ADMISSION INFO (2013/2014 PRICES)

Adult Standing: £15.00
Adult Seating: £15.00
Child/Senior Citizen Standing: £8.00
Child/Senior Citizen Seating: £8.00
Programme Price: £2.00

DISABLED INFORMATION

Wheelchairs: 24 spaces are available in the Disabled Area beneath the Family Stand
Helpers: One admitted per wheelchair
Prices: Free for one wheelchair plus helper
Disabled Toilets: Available in the Disabled Area
Are Bookings Necessary: Only for all ticket games
Contact: (01292) 263435

Travelling Supporters' Information:
Routes: Make for the A77 Ring Road around Ayr, exit via Whitletts Roundabout onto the A719 and follow the road towards Ayr. Just past the end of the racecourse, turn right at the traffic lights into Burnett Terrace, a sharp left and then right takes you into Somerset Road for the ground. (For car parking on Matchdays turn left at the traffic lights and then right 50 yards on into Craigie Park or on Somerset Road just past the ground on the left into Somerset Road car park).

BRECHIN CITY FC

Founded: 1906 (**Entered League**: 1923)
Nickname: 'The City'
Ground: Glebe Park, Trinity Road, Brechin, Angus, DD9 6BJ
Ground Capacity: 3,960
Seating Capacity: 1,519
Record Attendance: 9,123 (3rd February 1973)
Pitch Size: 110 × 67 yards
Colours: Red and White shirts and shorts
Telephone N°: (01356) 622856
Ticket Office: (01356) 622856
Fax Number: (01356) 625667
Secretary's Number: 07810 226224
Web Site: www.brechincity.com

GENERAL INFORMATION

Car Parking: Small Car Park at the ground and street parking
Coach Parking: Street parking
Nearest Railway Station: Montrose (8 miles)
Nearest Bus Station: Brechin
Club Shop: At the ground
Opening Times: Matchdays Only
Telephone N°: (01356) 622856

GROUND INFORMATION

Away Supporters' Entrances & Sections:
Main Stand – Trinity Road End

ADMISSION INFO (2013/2014 PRICES)

Adult Standing: £13.00
Adult Seating: £13.00
Concessionary Standing: £7.00
Concessionary Seating: £7.00
Parent & Child Ticket: £16.00
Note: Prices for visiting fans are higher than those shown
Programme Price: £2.00

DISABLED INFORMATION

Wheelchairs: 10 spaces each for home and away fans
Helpers: Please phone the club for details
Prices: Please phone the club for details
Disabled Toilets: Two available in the Covered Enclosure
Contact: (01356) 622856 (Bookings are not necessary)

Travelling Supporters' Information:
Routes: From the South and West: Take the M90 to the A94 and continue along past the first 'Brechin' turn-off. Take the second turn signposted 'Brechin'. On entering Brechin, the ground is on the left-hand side of the road between some houses.

DUNFERMLINE ATHLETIC FC

Founded: 1885 (**Entered League**: 1921)
Nickname: 'The Pars'
Ground: East End Park, Halbeath Road, Dunfermline, Fife, KY12 7RB
Ground Capacity: 11,780 (All seats)
Record Attendance: 27,816 (30th April 1968)
Pitch Size: 115 × 71 yards

Colours: Black and White shirts and shorts
Telephone No: (01383) 724295
Ticket Office: (01383) 745909
Fax Number: (01383) 741098
Web Site: www.dafc.co.uk
E-mail: enquiries@dafc.co.uk

GENERAL INFORMATION

Car Parking: Limited spaces in a Car Park at the ground.
Coach Parking: Leys Park Road
Nearest Railway Station: Dunfermline Queen Margaret (10 minutes walk)
Nearest Bus Station: Queen Anne Street, Dunfermline (10 minutes walk)
Club Shop: At the Ground
Opening Times: Monday to Saturday 9.00am – 5.30pm
Telephone No: (01383) 724295

GROUND INFORMATION

Away Supporters' Entrances & Sections:
Turnstiles 10-15 for the East Stand. Turnstiles 16-18 for the North East Stand

ADMISSION INFO (2013/2014 PRICES)

Adult Seating: £15.00 – £17.00
Under-18s/Other Concessions Seating: £10.00 – £12.00
Under-12s Seating: £5.00 – £7.00
Note: Match prices vary according to the category of game
Programme Price: £3.00

DISABLED INFORMATION

Wheelchairs: 12 spaces each for home & away fans
Helpers: One admitted per wheelchair
Prices: Concessionary prices for the wheelchair disabled. Helpers are admitted free of charge
Disabled Toilets: Available in West and East Stands and also in the Main Stand Hospitality Area
Contact: (01383) 745909 (Bookings are necessary – Away fans contact Kenny Arnott – kenny@dafc.co.uk)

Travelling Supporters' Information:
Routes: From the Forth Road Bridge and Perth: Exit the M90 at Junction 3 and take the A907 (Halbeath Road) into Dunfermline – the ground is on right; From Kincardine Bridge and Alloa: Take the A985 to the A994 into Dunfermline. Take Pittencrief Street, Glen Bridge and Carnegie Drive to Sinclair Gardens roundabout. Take the 1st exit toward the Traffic Lights then turn right into Ley's Park Road. Take the second exit on the right into the Car Park at the rear of the stadium.

EAST FIFE FC

Founded: 1903 (**Entered League**: 1903)
Nickname: 'The Fife'
Ground: Bayview Stadium, Harbour View, Methil, Fife KY8 3RW
Ground Capacity: 2,000 (All seats)
Record Attendance: 22,515 (2nd January 1950)
Pitch Size: 115 × 75 yards

Colours: Black and Gold striped shirts with Black shorts
Telephone Nº: (01333) 426323
Ticket Office: (01333) 426323
Fax Number: (01333) 426376
Web Site: www.eastfifefc.info
E-mail: office@eastfifefc.info

GENERAL INFORMATION

Car Parking: Adjacent to the ground
Coach Parking: Adjacent to the ground
Nearest Railway Station: Kirkcaldy (8 miles)
Nearest Bus Station: Leven
Club Shop: At the ground
Opening Times: Matchdays and normal office hours
Telephone Nº: (01333) 426323

GROUND INFORMATION

Away Supporters' Entrances & Sections:
Accommodated within the Main Stand

ADMISSION INFO (2013/2014 PRICES)

Adult Seating: £13.00
Child Seating: £5.00
Concessionary Seating: £10.00
Programme Price: £2.00

DISABLED INFORMATION

Wheelchairs: 24 spaces available in total
Helpers: Admitted
Prices: Normal prices charged for the disabled and helpers
Disabled Toilets: Yes
Contact: (01333) 426323 (Bookings are necessary)

Travelling Supporters' Information:
Routes: Take the A915 from Kirkcaldy past Buckhaven and Methil to Leven. Turn right at the traffic lights and go straight on at the first roundabout then turn right at the second roundabout. Cross Bawbee Bridge and turn left at the next roundabout. The ground is the first turning on the left after ¼ mile.

FORFAR ATHLETIC FC

Founded: 1885 (**Entered League**: 1921)
Nickname: 'Loons'
Ground: Station Park, Carseview Road, Forfar, Angus DD8 3BT
Ground Capacity: 6,038
Seating Capacity: 739
Record Attendance: 10,780 (2nd February 1970)

Pitch Size: 113 × 70 yards
Colours: Sky Blue shirts with Navy trim, Navy shorts
Telephone Nº: (01307) 463576
Ticket Office: (01307) 463576
Fax Number: (01307) 466951
Web Site: www.forfarathletic.co.uk

GENERAL INFORMATION

Car Parking: Market Muir Car Park and adjacent streets
Coach Parking: Market Muir Car Park
Nearest Railway Station: Dundee or Arbroath (14 miles)
Nearest Bus Station: Forfar (½ mile)
Club Shop: None

GROUND INFORMATION

Away Supporters' Entrances & Sections:
West End entrances for West End Terracing and North part of the Main Stand

ADMISSION INFO (2013/2014 PRICES)

Adult Standing: £12.00 – £14.00
Adult Seating: £13.00 – £15.00
Child/Senior Citizen Standing: £6.00 – £8.00
Child/Senior Citizen Seating: £7.00 – £8.00
Programme Price: £1.50

DISABLED INFORMATION

Wheelchairs: 4 spaces each for home and away fans accommodated to the west of the Main Stand
Helpers: Please phone the club for details
Prices: Please phone the club for details
Disabled Toilets: One available
Contact: (01307) 463576 (Bookings are necessary)

Travelling Supporters' Information:
Routes: Take the A85/M90 to Dundee and then the A929. Exit at the 2nd turn-off (signposted for Forfar). On the outskirts of Forfar, turn right at the T-junction and then left at the next major road. The ground is signposted on the left (down the cobbled street with the railway arch).

RANGERS FC

Founded: 1872 (**Entered League**: 1890)
Nickname: 'The Gers' 'Light Blues'
Ground: Ibrox Stadium, 150 Edmiston Drive, Glasgow G51 2XD
Ground Capacity: 50,987 (All seats)
Record Attendance: 118,567 (2nd January 1939)
Pitch Size: 115 × 72 yards

Colours: Shirts are Blue with White collar and White and Red trim, White shorts
Telephone Nº: 0871 702-1972
Ticket Office: 0871 702-1972
Fax Number: (0141) 580-8504
Web Site: www.rangers.co.uk

GENERAL INFORMATION

Car Parking: Albion Car Park
Coach Parking: By Police direction
Away fans Car/Coach Parking: Broomloan Road
Nearest Underground Station: Ibrox (2 minutes walk)
Nearest Bus Station: Glasgow City Centre
Club Shop: JJB Rangers Megastore, Ibrox Stadium
Opening Times: Monday to Friday 9.00am to 5.30pm, Saturdays 9.00am – 3.00pm and closed on Sundays. Opening hours may vary depending on match times
Megastore Telephone Nº: (0141) 427-4444

GROUND INFORMATION

Away Supporters' Entrances & Sections:
Govan West Corner and turnstiles

ADMISSION INFO (2013/2014 PRICES)

Please contact the club for information about ticket pricing during the 2013/2014 season.
Note: Most of the seats are taken by season ticket holders
Programme Price: £3.00

DISABLED INFORMATION

Wheelchairs: 65 spaces for home fans in front of the West Enclosure, 7 spaces for away fans in the Govan West Stand and 4 spaces for home fans in the Broomloan Stand
Helpers: Admitted
Prices: Free of charge for the disabled and helpers if they are Wheelchair season ticket holders or M2M members. Please contact the Club for further information.
Disabled Toilets: Available in the East and West Enclosures, Govan West Stand, Argyle House, Main Stand & Broomloan Front
Contact: 0871 702-1972 (Bookings are necessary)

Travelling Supporters' Information:
Routes: From All Parts: Exit the M8 at Junction 23. The road leads straight to the Stadium.

STENHOUSEMUIR FC

Founded: 1884 (**Entered League**: 1921)
Former Names: Heather Rangers FC
Nickname: 'Warriors'
Ground: Ochilview Park, Gladstone Road, Stenhousemuir FK5 4QL
Ground Capacity: 3,096 **Seating Capacity**: 626
Record Attendance: 12,500 (11th March 1950)

Pitch Size: 110 × 72 yards
Colours: Maroon shirts and shorts
Telephone Nº: (01324) 562992
Ticket Office: (01324) 562992
Fax Number: (01324) 562980
Web Site: www.stenhousemuirfc.com
E-mail: secretary@stranraerfc.org

GENERAL INFORMATION

Car Parking: A Large Car Park is adjacent
Coach Parking: Tryst Showground (adjacent)
Nearest Railway Station: Larbert (1 mile)
Nearest Bus Station: Falkirk (2½ miles)
Club Shop: At the ground
Opening Times: Weekdays from 9.00am to 5.00pm (closed on Wednesday afternoons) and from 2.00pm on Saturday matchdays
Telephone Nº: (01324) 562992

GROUND INFORMATION

Away Supporters' Entrances & Sections: Terracing entrances and accommodation

ADMISSION INFO (2013/2014 PRICES)

Adult Standing: £12.00
Adult Seating: £13.00
Senior Citizen/Child/Concessionary Standing: £7.00
Senior Citizen/Child/Concessionary Seating: £8.00
Note: Prices may differ for the fixtures against Rangers FC.
Programme Price: £2.00

DISABLED INFORMATION

Wheelchairs: Accommodated
Helpers: Admitted
Prices: Normal prices are charged
Disabled Toilets: Available in the Gladstone Road Stand
Contact: (01324) 562992 (Bookings are not necessary)

Travelling Supporters' Information:
Routes: Exit the M876 at Junction 2 and follow signs for Stenhousemuir. Pass the Old Hospital and turn right after the Golf Course. The ground is on the left behind the houses – the floodlights are visible for ¼ mile.

STRANRAER FC

Founded: 1870 (**Entered League**: 1955)
Nickname: 'The Blues'
Ground: Stair Park, London Road, Stranraer, DG9 8BS
Ground Capacity: 5,600
Seating Capacity: 1,830
Record Attendance: 6,500 (24th January 1948)

Pitch Size: 112 × 70 yards
Colours: Blue shirts with White shorts
Telephone Nº: (01776) 703271
Ticket Office: (01776) 703271
Web Site: www.stranraerfc.org
E-mail: secretary@stranraerfc.org

GENERAL INFORMATION

Car Parking: Car Park at the ground
Coach Parking: Port Rodie, Stranraer
Nearest Railway Station: Stranraer (1 mile)
Nearest Bus Station: Port Rodie, Stranraer
Club Shop: At the ground
Opening Times: 2.15pm to 3.00pm and during half-time on Matchdays only
Telephone Nº: None

GROUND INFORMATION

Away Supporters' Entrances & Sections:
London Road entrances for the Visitors Stand

ADMISSION INFO (2013/2014 PRICES)

Adult Standing: £13.00 – £18.00
Adult Seating: £13.00 – £18.00
Under-16s Standing: £5.00 – £7.00
Under-16s Seating: £5.00 – £7.00
Concessionary Standing: £7.00 – £9.00
Concessionary Seating: £7.00 – £9.00
Note: The above prices may be subject to change.
Programme Price: £2.00

DISABLED INFORMATION

Wheelchairs: 6 spaces each for Home and Away fans in front of the North Stand and South Stand
Helpers: Please phone the club for details
Prices: Please phone the club for details
Disabled Toilets: One in the North and South Stands
Contact: (01776) 703271 (Bookings are necessary)

Travelling Supporters' Information:
Routes: From the West: Take the A75 to Stranraer and the ground is on the left-hand side of the road in a public park shortly after entering the town; From the North: Take the A77 and follow it to where it joins with the A75 (then as West). The ground is set back from the road and the floodlights are clearly visible.

The Scottish Professional Football League – Division Three

Address
National Stadium, Hampden Park,
Mount Florida, Glasgow G42 9DE

Phone (0141) 620-4140
Fax (0141) 620-4141

Clubs for the 2013/2014 Season

ALBION ROVERS FC

Founded: 1882 (Entered League: 1903)
Nickname: 'Wee Rovers'
Ground: Cliftonhill Stadium, Main Street, Coatbridge, Lanarkshire ML5 3RB
Ground Capacity: 1,238
Seating Capacity: 538
Record Attendance: 27,381 (8th February 1936)

Pitch Size: 110 × 72 yards
Colours: Red and Yellow shirts with Red shorts
Telephone N°: (01236) 606334
Ticket Office: (01236) 606334
Fax Number: (01236) 606334
Web Site: www.albionroversfc.com
E-mail: info@albionroversfc.com

GENERAL INFORMATION

Car Parking: Street parking and Albion Street
Coach Parking: Street parking only
Nearest Railway Station: Coatdyke (10 minutes walk)
Nearest Bus Station: Coatbridge
Club Shop: At the ground
Opening Times: One hour before each home match
Telephone N°: (01236) 606334

GROUND INFORMATION

Away Supporters' Entrances & Sections:
Main Street entrance for the Main Street Area

ADMISSION INFO (2013/2014 PRICES)

Adult Standing: £10.00
Adult Seating: £10.00
Student/Senior Citizen Standing/Seating: £5.00
Under-16s Standing/Seating: Free if accompanied by a paying adult. Otherwise £2.00
Programme Price: £2.00

DISABLED INFORMATION

Wheelchairs: Approximately 30 spaces available in the Disabled Area
Helpers: Admitted
Prices: Free of charge for disabled fans and their helpers
Disabled Toilets: Available at the East End of the Ground
Contact: (01236) 606334 (Bookings are advisable)

Travelling Supporters' Information:
Routes: From the East or West: Take the A8/M8 to the Shawhead Interchange then follow the A725 to the Town Centre. Follow A89 signs towards Airdrie at the roundabout, the ground is then on the left; From the South: Take the A725 from Bellshill/Hamilton/Motherwell/M74 to Coatbridge. Follow the A89 signs towards Airdrie at the roundabout, the ground is then on the left; From the North: Take the A73 to Airdrie then follow signs for the A8010 to Coatbridge. Join the A89 and the ground is one mile on the right.

ANNAN ATHLETIC FC

Founded: 1942
Former Names: Solway Star FC
Nickname: 'Galabankies'
Ground: Galabank, North Street, Annan, Dumfries & Galloway DG12 5DQ
Record Attendance: 1,500
Pitch Size: 110 × 66 yards

Ground Capacity: 3,000
Seating Capacity: 500
Colours: Black and Gold striped shirts, Black shorts
Telephone N°: (01461) 204108
Fax Number: (01461) 204108
Web Site: www.annanathleticfc.com
E-mail: annanathleticfc@aol.com

GENERAL INFORMATION

Car Parking: Available at the ground
Coach Parking: Available at the ground
Nearest Railway Station: Annan
Nearest Bus Station: Annan
Club Shop: At the ground
Opening Times: Saturdays between 3.00pm and 6.00pm
Telephone N°: (01461) 204108

GROUND INFORMATION

Away Supporters' Entrances & Sections:
North Stand

ADMISSION INFO (2013/2014 PRICES)

Adult Standing: £10.00 **Adult Seating**: £10.00
Child Standing: £5.00 **Child Seating**: £5.00
Note: Under-12s are admitted free of charge when accompanied by a paying adult
Programme Price: £1.50

DISABLED INFORMATION

Wheelchairs: Accommodated
Helpers: Please phone the club for details
Prices: Please phone the club for details
Disabled Toilets: Available
Contact: (01461) 204108 (Bookings are necessary)

Travelling Supporters' Information:
Routes: From the East: Take the A75 to Annan. Approaching Annan, exit onto the B6357 (Stapleton Road) and after ¾ mile take the second exit at the roundabout into Scotts Street. Continue into Church Street and High Street. Turn right into Lady Street (B722) and following along into North Street for the ground; From the West: Take the A75 to Annan and turn right onto the B721 through Howes and into High Street in Annan (1 mile). After about 300 yards turn left into Lady Street. Then as above.

BERWICK RANGERS FC

Founded: 1884 (**Entered League**: 1951)
Nickname: 'The Borderers'
Ground: Shielfield Park, Shielfield Terrace, Tweedmouth, Berwick-upon-Tweed TD15 2EF
Ground Capacity: 4,500
Seating Capacity: 1,224
Record Attendance: 13,365 (28th January 1967)
Pitch Size: 110 × 70 yards

Colours: Black shirts with a Gold panel, Black shorts
Telephone Nº: (01289) 307424
Ticket Office: (01289) 307424
Fax Number: (01289) 309424
Web Site: www.berwickrangersfc.co.uk
E-mail: club@berwickrangersfc.co.uk

GENERAL INFORMATION

Car Parking: Large Car Park at the ground
Coach Parking: At the ground
Nearest Railway Station: Berwick-upon-Tweed (1½ miles)
Nearest Bus Station: Berwick Town Centre (1 mile)
Club Shop: Inside the Stadium
Opening Times: Matchdays Only (+ On-line sales)
Telephone Nº: (01289) 307424

GROUND INFORMATION

Away Supporters' Entrances & Sections:
Shielfield Terrace entrance for the Popular Side Terrace (Gates A or B), Gate B for Main Stand accommodation. Gate A is only used for selected matches.

ADMISSION INFO (2013/2014 PRICES)

Adult Standing: £12.00
Adult Seating: £12.00
Concessionary Seating/Standing: £6.00
Programme Price: £2.00

DISABLED INFORMATION

Wheelchairs: Accommodated in the disabled section
Helpers: Admitted with wheelchair disabled
Prices: Please contact the club for pricing information
Disabled Toilets: Available between the turnstiles and the Grandstand entrance and behind the covered terracing. Also available in the Black & Gold Pub by the car park
Contact: (01289) 307424 (Bookings are recommended)

Travelling Supporters' Information:
Routes: From the North: Take the A1 (Berwick Bypass), cross the new road-bridge then take the 1st exit at the roundabout. Carry on for approximately ¼ mile to the next roundabout, go straight across then continue for approximately ¼ mile into Shielfield Terrace. Turn left and the ground is on the left; From the South: Take the A1 Bypass and continue across the first roundabout signposted Scremerston/Tweedmouth and then on for 1 mile. At the crossroads/junction take B6354 'Spittal' Road right and continue for approx. 1 mile until the road becomes Shielfield Terrace. The ground is on the left in Shielfield Terrace.

CLYDE FC

Founded: 1877 (**Entered League**: 1906)
Nickname: 'Bully Wee'
Ground: Broadwood Stadium, Cumbernauld, Glasgow G68 9NE
Ground Capacity: 8,200 (all seats)
Record Attendance: 8,000 (14th August 1996)
Pitch Size: 115 × 75 yards

Colours: White Shirts with Black piping, Black shorts
Telephone Nº: (01236) 451511
Ticket Office: (01236) 451511
Fax Number: (01236) 733490
Web Site: www.clydefc.co.uk
E-mail: info@clydefc.co.uk

GENERAL INFORMATION

Car Parking: Behind the Main and West Stands
Coach Parking: Behind the Main Stand
Nearest Railway Station: Croy (1½ miles)
Nearest Bus Station: Cumbernauld Town Centre
Club Shop: At the ground
Opening Times: One hour before and after the match
Telephone Nº: (01236) 451511

GROUND INFORMATION

Away Supporters' Entrances & Sections:
West Stand Turnstile for the West Stand area

ADMISSION INFO (2013/2014 PRICES)

Adult Seating: £12.00
Under-16s Seating: £2.00
Concessionary Seating: £6.00
Programme Price: £2.00

DISABLED INFORMATION

Wheelchairs: 10 spaces each for home and away fans accommodated in front sections of each stand
Helpers: One helper admitted per wheelchair
Prices: Free of charge for the disabled and helpers
Disabled Toilets: 4 available in the Main and West Stands
Contact: (01236) 451511 (Bookings are not necessary)

Travelling Supporters' Information:
Routes: From all Parts: Exit the A80 at Broadwood Junction and follow the signs for Broadwood. The ground is signposted from the next roundabout.

EAST STIRLINGSHIRE FC

East Stirlingshire are groundsharing with Stenhousemuir for the 2013/2014 season.

Founded: 1880 (**Entered League**: 1900)
Former Names: Bainsford Britannia FC
Nickname: 'The Shire'
Ground: Ochilview Park, Gladstone Road, Stenhousemuir FK5 5QL
Ground Capacity: 2,654
Seating Capacity: 628
Pitch Size: 110 × 72 yards

Record Attendance: 12,000 (21/2/1921 – Firs Park)
Colours: Black and White hooped shirts, Black shorts
Office Address: 81d Main Street, Bainsford, Falkirk, Stirlingshire FK2 7NZ
Telephone Nº: (01324) 629942
Fax Number: (01324) 629942
Web Site: www.eaststirlingshirefc.co.uk
E-mail: fceaststirlingshire@gmail.com

GENERAL INFORMATION

Car Parking: A large Car Park is adjacent
Coach Parking: Behind the North Terracing
Nearest Railway Station: Larbert (1 mile)
Nearest Bus Station: Falkirk (2½ miles)
Club Shop: At the office (see above for details)
Opening Times: Weekdays from 10.00am to 3.00pm
Telephone Nº: (01324) 629942

GROUND INFORMATION

Away Supporters' Entrances & Sections:
No usual segregation

ADMISSION INFO (2013/2014 PRICES)

Adult Standing: £10.00
Adult Seating: £10.00
Child/Senior Citizen Standing: £5.00
Child/Senior Citizen Seating: £5.00
Programme Price: £2.00

DISABLED INFORMATION

Wheelchairs: Accommodated
Helpers: Admitted
Prices: £5.00 for the disabled. Helpers admitted free.
Disabled Toilets: Available in the Main Stand
Contact: (01324) 629942 (Bookings are necessary)

Travelling Supporters' Information:
Routes: Exit the M876 at Junction 2 and follow signs for Stenhousemuir. Pass the Old Hospital and turn right after the Golf Course. The ground is on the left behind the houses – the floodlights are visible for ¼ mile.

ELGIN CITY FC

Founded: 1893 (**Entered League**: 2000)
Nickname: 'Black and Whites'
Ground: Borough Briggs, Borough Briggs Road, Elgin IV30 1AP
Ground Capacity: 3,716
Seating Capacity: 478
Record Attendance: 12,640 (17th February 1968)
Pitch Size: 120 × 86 yards
Colours: Black and White shirts with Black shorts
Telephone Nº: (01343) 551114
Ticket Information: (01343) 551114
Fax Number: (01343) 547921
Web Site: www.elgincity.com
E-mail: office@elgincity.com

GENERAL INFORMATION

Car Parking: At the ground
Coach Parking: At the ground
Nearest Railway Station: Elgin (1 mile)
Nearest Bus Station: Elgin (¼ mile)
Club Shop: At the ground
Opening Times: Weekdays 9.30am to 4.30pm and also Saturdays 10.00am to 5.00pm (home matchdays only)
Telephone Nº: (01343) 551114

GROUND INFORMATION

Away Supporters' Entrances & Sections:
West End entrances for the Covered Enclosure

ADMISSION INFO (2013/2014 PRICES)

Adult Standing: £10.00
Adult Seating: £12.00
Child/Senior Citizen Standing: £5.00
Child/Senior Citizen Seating: £7.00
Programme Price: £2.00

DISABLED INFORMATION

Wheelchairs: Accommodated
Helpers: Admitted
Prices: The disabled are admitted at concessionary prices
Disabled Toilets: Available
Contact: (01343) 551114 (Bookings are not necessary)

Travelling Supporters' Information:
Routes: Take the Alexandra bypass to the roundabout ½ mile from the City Centre and turn left towards Lossiemouth. Borough Briggs Road is on the left.

MONTROSE FC

Founded: 1879 (**Entered League**: 1929)
Nickname: 'Gable Endies'
Ground: Links Park Stadium, Wellington Street, Montrose DD10 8QD
Ground Capacity: 4,936
Seating Capacity: 1,338
Record Attendance: 8,983 (vs Dundee – 17/3/1973)

Pitch Size: 113 × 70 yards
Colours: Royal Blue shirts with Blue shorts
Telephone Nº: (01674) 673200
Ticket Office: (01674) 673200
Fax Number: (01674) 677311
Web Site: www.montrosefc.co.uk
E-mail: montrosefootballclub@tesco.net

GENERAL INFORMATION

Car Parking: At the ground and Street parking also
Coach Parking: Mid-Links
Nearest Railway Station: Montrose Western Road
Nearest Bus Station: High Street, Montrose
Club Shop: At the ground
Opening Times: Matchdays 10.00am to 3.00pm and also on Monday and Wednesday evenings
Telephone Nº: (01674) 673200

GROUND INFORMATION

Away Supporters' Entrances & Sections:
No usual segregation

ADMISSION INFO (2013/2014 PRICES)

Adult Standing: £11.00
Adult Seating: £11.00
Child Standing: £6.00
Child Seating: £6.00
Programme Price: £2.00

DISABLED INFORMATION

Wheelchairs: 5 spaces available in the Main Stand
Helpers: Please phone the club for information
Prices: Please phone the club for information
Disabled Toilets: 2 available in the Main Stand
Contact: (01674) 673200 (Bookings are helpful)

Travelling Supporters' Information:
Routes: Take the main A92 Coastal Road to Montrose. Once in the town, the ground is well signposted and is situated in the Mid-Links area.

PETERHEAD FC

Founded: 1891 (**Entered League**: 2000)
Nickname: 'Blue Toon'
Ground: Balmoor Stadium, Peterhead AB42 1EU
Ground Capacity: 3,300
Seating Capacity: 980
Record Attendance: 2,300
Pitch Size: 110 × 70 yards

Colours: Shirts and Shorts are Royal Blue with White piping
Telephone Nº: (01779) 478256
Fax Number: (01779) 490682
Web Site: www.peterheadfc.co.uk
E-mail: office@peterheadfc.co.uk

GENERAL INFORMATION

Car Parking: At the ground
Coach Parking: At the ground
Nearest Railway Station: Aberdeen
Nearest Bus Station: Peterhead
Club Shop: At the ground
Opening Times: Monday to Saturday 9.00am to 5.00pm
Telephone Nº: (01779) 478256

GROUND INFORMATION

Away Supporters' Entrances & Sections:
Segregation only used when required which is very rare

ADMISSION INFO (2013/2014 PRICES)

Adult Standing: £12.00
Adult Seating: £14.00
Child/Concessionary Standing: £6.00
Child/Concessionary Seating: £7.00
Programme Price: £2.00

DISABLED INFORMATION

Wheelchairs: Accommodated
Helpers: Please phone the club for details
Prices: Please phone the club for details
Disabled Toilets: Available
Contact: (01779) 473434 (Bookings are necessary)

Travelling Supporters' Information:
Routes: The ground is situated on the left of the main road from Fraserburgh (A952), 300 yards past the swimming pool.

QUEEN'S PARK FC

Founded: 1867 (**Entered League**: 1900)
Nickname: 'The Spiders'
Ground: Hampden Park, Mount Florida, Glasgow, G42 9BA
Ground Capacity: 52,000 (All seats)
Record Attendance: 150,239 (17th April 1937)

Pitch Size: 115 × 75 yards
Colours: Black and White hooped shirts, White shorts
Telephone/Ticket Office Nº: (0141) 632-1275
Fax Number: (0141) 636-1612
Web Site: www.queensparkfc.co.uk
E-mail: secretary@queensparkfc.co.uk

GENERAL INFORMATION

Car Parking: Car Park at the Stadium
Coach Parking: Car Park at the Stadium
Nearest Railway Station: Mount Florida and King's Park (both 5 minutes walk)
Nearest Bus Station: Buchanan Street
Club Shop: At the ground
Opening Times: During home matches only
Telephone Nº: (0141) 632-1275

GROUND INFORMATION

Away Supporters' Entrances & Sections: South Stand

ADMISSION INFO (2013/2014 PRICES)

Adult Seating: £12.00
Concessionary Seating: £2.00
Family Ticket: £13.00 for a parent and then an extra £1.00 for each accompanied child
Programme Price: £2.00
Note: Only the South Stand is presently used for games

DISABLED INFORMATION

Wheelchairs: 160 spaces available in total
Helpers: Admitted
Prices: Free for the disabled. Helpers normal prices
Disabled Toilets: Available
Contact: (0141) 632-1275 (Bookings are necessary)

Travelling Supporters' Information:
Routes: From the South: Take the A724 to the Cambuslang Road and at Eastfield branch left into Main Street and follow through Burnhill Street and Westmuir Place into Prospecthill Road. Turn left into Aikenhead Road and right into Mount Annan for Kinghorn Drive and the Stadium; From the South: Take the A77 Fenwick Road, through Kilmarnock Road into Pollokshaws Road then turn right into Langside Avenue. Pass through Battle Place to Battlefield Road and turn left into Cathcart Road. Turn right into Letherby Drive, right into Carmunnock Road and 1st left into Mount Annan Drive for the Stadium; From the North & East: Exit M8 Junction 15 and passing Infirmary on left proceed into High Street and cross the Albert Bridge into Crown Street. Join Cathcart Road and proceed South until it becomes Carmunnock Road. Turn left into Mount Annan Drive and left again into Kinghorn Drive for the Stadium.

STIRLING ALBION FC

Founded: 1945 (**Entered League**: 1946)
Nickname: 'The Binos'
Ground: Forth Bank Stadium, Springkerse, Stirling, FK7 7UJ
Ground Capacity: 3,808
Seating Capacity: 2,508
Record Attendance: 3,808 (17th February 1996)

Pitch Size: 110 × 74 yards
Colours: Shirts are Red with White sleeves, Red Shorts
Telephone N°: (01786) 450399
Ticket Office: (01786) 450399
Fax Number: (01786) 448592
Web site: www.stirlingalbionfc.co.uk
E-mail: stirlingalbion@btconnect.com

GENERAL INFORMATION

Car Parking: At the ground
Coach Parking: Adjacent to the ground
Nearest Railway Station: Stirling (2 miles)
Nearest Bus Station: Stirling (2 miles)
Club Shop: At the ground
Opening Times: Weekdays and Matchdays from 10.00am to 4.00pm
Telephone N°: (01786) 450399

GROUND INFORMATION

Away Supporters' Entrances & Sections:
South Terracing and East Stand

ADMISSION INFO (2013/2014 PRICES)

Adult Standing/Seating: £10.00
Concessionary Standing/Seating: £7.00
Under-17s Standing/Seating: £5.00
Note: Standing admission is only available for certain games.
Programme Price: £2.00

DISABLED INFORMATION

Wheelchairs: 18 spaces each for home and away fans
Helpers: Admitted
Prices: Free of charge for the disabled and helpers
Disabled Toilets: 2 available beneath each stand
Contact: (01786) 450399 (Bookings are necessary)

Travelling Supporters' Information:
Routes: Follow signs for Stirling from the M9/M80 Northbound. From Pirnhall Roundabout follow signs for Alloa/St. Andrew's to the 4th roundabout and then turn left for the stadium.

THE HIGHLAND FOOTBALL LEAGUE

Founded 1893

Secretary Mr J.H. Grant

Contact Address
35 Hamilton Drive, Elgin IV30 2NN

Phone (01343) 544995

Web site www.highlandfootballleague.com

Clubs for the 2013/2014 Season

BRORA RANGERS FC

Founded: 1878
Nickname: 'The Cattachs'
Ground: Dudgeon Park Road, Brora KW9 6QH
Ground Capacity: 2,000
Seating Capacity: 200
Record Attendance: 2,000 (31st August 1963)
Web site: www.brorarangers.co.uk

Colours: Shirts are Red with White underarm flashes, Shorts are Red
Telephone/Fax Nº: (01408) 621231
Social Club Phone Nº: (01408) 621570
Contact Phone Nº: (01408) 621114
Correspondence Address: Kevin Mackay, 2 Muirfield Road, Brora KW9 6QP

GENERAL INFORMATION

Car Parking: Adjacent to the ground
Coach Parking: Adjacent to the ground
Nearest Railway Station: Brora
Nearest Bus Station: Brora
Club Shop: At the ground
Opening Times: Matchdays only
Telephone Nº: (01408) 621231

GROUND INFORMATION

Away Supporters' Entrances & Sections:
No usual segregation

ADMISSION INFO (2013/2014 PRICES)

Adult Standing: £6.00
Adult Seating: £7.00
Child Standing: £3.00
Child Seating: £4.00
Note: Under-14s are admitted free with a paying adult
Programme Price: £1.00

DISABLED INFORMATION

Wheelchairs: Accommodated
Helpers: Please phone the club for details
Prices: Please phone the club for details
Disabled Toilets: None at present (under construction)
Contact: (01408) 621231 (Bookings are necessary)

Travelling Supporters' Information:
Routes: Take the A9 Northbound from Inverness and the Stadium is situated on the right upon entering the town. It is clearly visible from the road.

BUCKIE THISTLE FC

Founded: 1889
Former Names: None
Nickname: 'The Jags'
Ground: New Victoria Park, Midmar Street, Buckie, AB56 1BJ
Pitch Size: 109 × 73 yards
Record Attendance: 8,168 (1st March 1958)
Ground Capacity: 3,000
Seating Capacity: 400
Colours: Green and White hooped shirts, White shorts
Telephone Nº: (01542) 831454
Web Site: www.buckiethistle.com

GENERAL INFORMATION

Car Parking: Adjacent to the ground
Coach Parking: Adjacent to the ground
Nearest Railway Station: Keith (12 miles)
Nearest Bus Station: Buckie
Club Shop: In the Supporters' Club inside the ground
Social Club: Victoria Park Function Hall at the ground
Social Club Telephone Nº: (01542) 831454

GROUND INFORMATION

Away Supporters' Entrances & Sections:
No usual segregation

ADMISSION INFO (2013/2014 PRICES)

Adult Standing: £8.00
Adult Seating: £8.00
Concessionary Standing/Seating: £4.00
Note: Under-14s are admitted free with a paying adult
Programme Price: £2.00

DISABLED INFORMATION

Wheelchairs: Accommodated in front of the stand
Helpers: Admitted
Prices: Normal prices apply
Disabled Toilets: Available in the Victoria Park Function Hall
Contact: (01542) 831454 (Bookings are helpful)

Travelling Supporters' Information:
Routes: From the East and West: Exit the A98 onto the A942 towards Buckie. Go straight on at the roundabout and travel along Buckie High Street. Turn left at the roundabout next to Cluny Square into West Church Street then take the 1st left into South Pringle Street. The ground is straight ahead.

CLACHNACUDDIN FC

Founded: 1886
Nickname: 'Lilywhites'
Ground: Grant Street Park, Wyvis Place, Inverness, IV3 6DR
Ground Capacity: 1,200
Seating Capacity: 154
Record Attendance: 9,000 (27th August 1951)
Pitch Size: 108 × 70 yards

Colours: White shirts with Black shorts
Telephone N°: (01463) 230860
Fax Number: (01463) 718261
Contact Address: c/o Highland Consultants, Corrie Lodge, Millburn Road, Inverness IV2 3TP
Contact Phone N°: 07756 669637
Web site: www.clachnacuddin.com

GENERAL INFORMATION

Car Parking: Adjacent to the ground
Coach Parking: Adjacent to the ground
Nearest Railway Station: Inverness
Nearest Bus Station: Inverness
Club Shop: At the ground
Opening Times: Matchdays only
Telephone N°: (01463) 718261

GROUND INFORMATION

Away Supporters' Entrances & Sections:
No usual segregation

ADMISSION INFO (2013/2014 PRICES)

Adult Standing: £6.00
Adult Seating: £7.00
Child Standing: £3.00
Child Seating: £4.00
Note: Under-14s are admitted free with a paying adult

DISABLED INFORMATION

Wheelchairs: Accommodated
Helpers: Admitted
Prices: Normal prices apply
Disabled Toilets: Available
Contact: (01463) 224706 (Bookings are not necessary)

Travelling Supporters' Information:
Routes: From the East and South: From the roundabout at the junction of the A9 and A96, proceed into the Town Centre and over the River Ness. Turn right at the traffic lights (onto the A862 to Dingwall), go up Kenneth Street and over the roundabout onto Telford Street for 200 yards before turning right into Telford Road opposite the Fish Shop. At the top, turn left onto Lower Kessack Street and left again. Finally, turn left into Wyvis Place and the ground is on the left.

COVE RANGERS FC

Founded: 1922
Nickname: None
Ground: Allan Park, Loirston Road, Cove, Aberdeen, AB12 3NR
Ground Capacity: 2,300
Seating Capacity: 100
Record Attendance: 2,300 (15th November 1992)
Pitch Size: 101 × 60 yards

Colours: Blue shirts and shorts
Telephone Nº: (01224) 871467 (Social Club)
Fax Number: (01224) 896282
Contact Address: Duncan Little, c/o Club
Contact Phone Nº: (01224) 890433 (Matchdays) or (01224) 896282 (Evenings)
Social Club Nº: (01224) 871467
Web Site: coverangers.uacstudios.com

GENERAL INFORMATION

Car Parking: School Car Park/Loirston Road
Coach Parking: By Police direction
Nearest Railway Station: Guild Street, Aberdeen
Nearest Bus Station: Guild Street, Aberdeen
Club Shop: At the Social Club
Opening Times: Matchdays Only
Telephone Nº: (01224) 871467

GROUND INFORMATION

Away Supporters' Entrances & Sections:
Loirston Road entrances and accommodation

ADMISSION INFO (2013/2014 PRICES)

Adult Standing: £8.00
Adult Seating: £8.00
Child Standing: £4.00
Child Seating: £4.00
Note: Under-14s are admitted free with a paying adult
Programme Price: £1.00

DISABLED INFORMATION

Wheelchairs: Accommodated
Helpers: Admitted
Prices: Free of charge for the disabled
Disabled Toilets: Available in the Social Club
Are Bookings Necessary: No, but preferable
Contact: (01224) 890433 (Duncan Little) (Matchdays); (01224) 896282 (Evenings)

Travelling Supporters' Information:
Routes: From the North: Follow signs to Altens and Cove and take the Cove turn-off at the Altens Thistle Hotel roundabout along Loirston Road – the ground is ½ mile on the right; From the South: Take the Aberdeen Harbour turn-off some 10 miles north of Stonehaven and continue to Altens Thistle Hotel roundabout – then as from the North.
Bus Routes: No. 13 bus runs from the City Centre to the ground.

DEVERONVALE FC

Founded: 1938
Nickname: 'The Vale'
Ground: Princess Royal Park, 56 Airlie Gardens, Banff AB45 1AZ
Ground Capacity: 2,651
Seating Capacity: 372
Record Attendance: 5,000 (27th April 1952)
Pitch Size: 109 × 78 yards

Colours: Shirts are Red with White trim, White shorts
Telephone Nº: (01261) 818303
Fax Number: (01261) 813753
Contact Address: Stewart McPherson, 8 Victoria Place, Banff AB45 1EL
Contact Phone Nº: (01261) 818303
Web Site: www.deveronvale.co.uk
E-mail: deveronvalefc@highlandleague.com

GENERAL INFORMATION

Car Parking: Adjacent to the ground plus street parking.
Coach Parking: Bridge Road Car Park
Nearest Railway Station: Keith (20 miles)
Nearest Bus Station: Macduff (1 mile)
Club Shop: At the ground
Opening Times: Matchdays only
Telephone Nº: (01261) 818303

GROUND INFORMATION

Away Supporters' Entrances & Sections:
No usual segregation

ADMISSION INFO (2013/2014 PRICES)

Adult Standing: £8.00
Adult Seating: £10.00
Child Standing: £4.00
Child Seating: £6.00
Note: Under-14s are admitted free with a paying adult

DISABLED INFORMATION

Wheelchairs: Accommodated
Helpers: Admitted
Prices: Please phone the club for details
Disabled Toilets: Available
Contact: (01261) 818303 (Bookings are necessary)

Travelling Supporters' Information:
Routes: From Aberdeen: Enter the town at Banff Bridge – the ground is situated ¼ mile along on the right; From Inverness: Travel through Banff on the main bypass and the ground is situated on the left, ¼ mile before Banff Bridge.

FORMARTINE UNITED FC

Founded: 1946
Nickname: 'United'
Ground: North Lodge Park, Pitmedden AB41 7XA
Ground Capacity: 1,800
Seating Capacity: 300
Record Attendance: 1,500

Colours: Red & White striped shirts with White shorts
Telephone Nº: (01651) 843266 (Matchdays only)
Contact Address: Martin Johnston, Tillygonnie, Riverside Road, Methlick AB41 7HN
Contact Phone Nº: (01651) 806604
Web site: www.formartineutd.com

GENERAL INFORMATION

Car Parking: At the ground
Coach Parking: At the ground
Nearest Railway Station: Inverurie (11 miles)
Nearest Bus Station: Inverurie
Club Shop: At Intersport in Ellon
Opening Times: Monday to Saturday 9.00am to 5.00pm

GROUND INFORMATION

Away Supporters' Entrances & Sections:
No usual segregation

ADMISSION INFO (2013/2014 PRICES)

Adult Standing: £8.00
Adult Seating: £8.00
Concessionary Standing/Seating: £4.00
Under-12s Standing/Seating: £4.00
Note: Under-14s are admitted free with a paying adult
Programme Price: £2.00

DISABLED INFORMATION

Wheelchairs: Accommodated
Helpers: Admitted with prior notice
Prices: Normal prices apply for the disabled and helpers
Disabled Toilets: Available
Contact: (01651) 806604 (Bookings are not necessary)

Travelling Supporters' Information:
Routes: Pitmedden is located approximately 15 miles north of Aberdeen on the A920 between Oldmeldrum and Ellon. North Lodge Park is situated just to the west of Pitmedden by the junction of the A920 and the B9000 which heads into Pitmedden itself.

FORRES MECHANICS FC

Founded: 1884
Nickname: 'Can Cans'
Ground: Mosset Park, Lea Road, Forres IV36 1AU
Ground Capacity: 1,400
Seating Capacity: 540
Record Attendance: 7,000 (2nd February 1957)
Pitch Size: 106 × 69 yards

Colours: Maroon & Gold striped shirts, Maroon shorts
Telephone/Fax Number: (01309) 675096
Contact Address: David W. Macdonald, Secretary, 7 Brinuth Place, Elgin IV30 6YW
Contact Phone Nº: (01343) 544294
Mobile Phone Contact Nº: 07779 782799
Web site: www.forresmechanics.net

GENERAL INFORMATION

Car Parking: At the ground
Coach Parking: At the ground
Nearest Railway Station: Forres
Nearest Bus Station: Forres
Club Shop: At the ground
Opening Times: Matchdays only
Telephone Nº: (01309) 675096

GROUND INFORMATION

Away Supporters' Entrances & Sections:
No usual segregation

ADMISSION INFO (2013/2014 PRICES)

Adult Standing: £6.00 **Adult Seating**: £8.00
Child/Senior Citizen Standing: £3.00
Child/Senior Citizen Seating: £4.00
Note: Under-14s are admitted free with a paying adult
Programme Price: £1.00

DISABLED INFORMATION

Wheelchairs: Accommodated
Helpers: Admitted
Prices: Normal prices apply
Disabled Toilets: One available
Contact: (01309) 675096 (Bookings are not necessary)

Travelling Supporters' Information:
Routes: From A96 East (Inverness): Turn off the A96 onto the B9011. Continue along this road and pass Tesco, turn left at the roundabout then immediately right into Inverene Road. Follow for about ½ mile then turn right across Lea Bridge then left for the ground; From A96 West (Aberdeen): Drive into Forres on the A96 passing the ground on your left. After a short distance, turn left onto the A940 (Market Street). Immediately before the roundabout turn left into Invererne Road. Then as above.

FORT WILLIAM FC

Founded: 1984
Nickname: 'The Fort'
Ground: Achintee Road, Fort William PH33 6TE
Ground Capacity: 4,000
Seating Capacity: 400
Record Attendance: 1,500 (4th January 1986)

Pitch Size: 103 × 70 yards
Colours: Yellow shirts with Black shorts
Telephone Nº: (01397) 698003
Contact Address: John Watssman, c/o Club
Contact Phone Nº: 07747 892661
Web site: www.fortwilliamfc.co.uk

GENERAL INFORMATION

Car Parking: At the ground
Coach Parking: At the ground
Nearest Railway Station: Fort William
Nearest Bus Station: Fort William
Club Shop: Sales via the club's web site

GROUND INFORMATION

Away Supporters' Entrances & Sections:
No usual segregation

ADMISSION INFO (2013/2014 PRICES)

Adult Standing: £7.00 **Adult Seating**: £8.00
Concessionary Standing: £3.50
Concessionary Seating: £3.50
Note: Under-14s are admitted free with a paying adult
Programme Price: No programme is produced

DISABLED INFORMATION

Wheelchairs: Accommodated in the stand
Helpers: Please phone the club for details
Prices: Concessionary prices apply for the disabled
Disabled Toilets: None at present
Contact: 07747 892661 (Bookings are not necessary)

Travelling Supporters' Information:
Routes: From the South: Approaching Fort William on the A82, proceed on the bypass of the Town Centre. After 2 roundabouts continue on Belford Road past the Railway Station on the left and the Swimming Baths on the right. After ½ mile and crossing over the River Nevis, take the first right into Claggan Road and the ground is ½ mile on the left; From Inverness: Take the A98 into Fort William before taking the 2nd left after the Shell petrol into Claggan Road. Take the 1st right before Spar signposted for the Ben Nevis Footpath. The ground is 1st left opposite the footbridge.

FRASERBURGH FC

Founded: 1910
Nickname: 'The Broch'
Ground: Bellslea Park, Seaforth Street, Fraserburgh, AB43 9BB
Ground Capacity: 1,480
Seating Capacity: 300
Record Attendance: 5,800 (13th February 1954)
Pitch Size: 110 × 72 yards (101 × 60 metres)

Colours: Black and White striped shirts, Black shorts
Telephone Nº: (01346) 518444
Contact Address: Finlay Noble, 18 Bawdley Head, Fraserburgh AB43 9SE
Contact Phone Nº: (01346) 518444
Mobile Phone Contact Nº: 07852 178634
Web Site: www.fraserburghfc.co.uk
E-mail: finlay.noble@fraserburghfc.co.uk

GENERAL INFORMATION

Car Parking: At the ground
Coach Parking: At the ground
Nearest Railway Station: Aberdeen (40 miles)
Nearest Bus Station: Fraserburgh
Club Shop: Designs On You, Commerce Street, Fraserburgh
Opening Times: Monday to Saturday 9.00am to 5.00pm
Telephone Nº: (01346) 512756

GROUND INFORMATION

Away Supporters' Entrances & Sections:
No usual segregation

ADMISSION INFO (2013/2014 PRICES)

Adult Standing: £8.00
Adult Seating: £9.00
Child Standing: £4.00
Child Seating: £5.00
Note: Under-14s are admitted free with a paying adult
Programme Price: £1.50

DISABLED INFORMATION

Wheelchairs: Accommodated
Helpers: Admitted
Prices: Normal prices apply
Disabled Toilets: Available
Contact: (01346) 518444 (Bookings are not necessary)

Travelling Supporters' Information:
Routes: The ground is situated in the Town Centre, off Seaforth Street.

HUNTLY FC

Founded: 1928
Nickname: None
Ground: Christie Park, East Park Street, Huntly, Aberdeenshire AB54 8JE
Ground Capacity: 2,480
Seating Capacity: 270
Record Attendance: 4,500 (18th February 1995)
Pitch Size: 105 × 72 yards

Colours: Black and Gold shirts with Black shorts
Telephone Nº: (01466) 793548
Social Club Phone Nº: (01466) 793680
Contact Address: Alix Turner, 12 Forest Way, Huntly, AB54 8RG
Contact Phone Nº: (01466) 793548
Web Site: www.huntlyfc.co.uk
E-mail: huntlyfc@highlandleague.com

GENERAL INFORMATION

Car Parking: At the ground
Coach Parking: At the ground
Nearest Railway Station: Huntly (1 mile)
Nearest Bus Station: Huntly (¼ mile)
Club Shop: At the ground
Opening Times: Matchdays only

GROUND INFORMATION

Away Supporters' Entrances & Sections:
No usual segregation

ADMISSION INFO (2013/2014 PRICES)

Adult Standing: £8.00
Adult Seating: £9.00
Child/Concessionary Standing: £5.00
Child/Concessionary Seating: £6.00
Note: Two Under-14s are admitted free with a paying adult
Programme Price: £1.50

DISABLED INFORMATION

Wheelchairs: Accommodated
Helpers: Admitted at normal prices
Prices: Concessionary prices apply for the disabled
Disabled Toilets: Available
Contact: (01466) 793269 (Bookings are not necessary)

Travelling Supporters' Information:
Routes: Enter Town off the A96 and proceed along King George V Avenue and Gordon Street. Pass through the Town Centre Square, along Castle Street to East Park Street and the ground is on the right before the Castle.

INVERURIE LOCO WORKS FC

Founded: 1903
Nickname: 'Locos'
Ground: Harlaw Park, Harlaw Road, Inverurie, AB51 4SR
Ground Capacity: 2,500
Seating Capacity: 250
Record Attendance: 2,150
Pitch Size: 110 × 70 yards

Colours: Red and Black striped shirts, Black shorts
Telephone Nº: 07500 664434
Fax Number: (01467) 622168
Contact Address: Billy Thomson, c/o Club
Contact Phone Nº: 0779 903-7640
Web Site: www.inverurielocoworks.com

GENERAL INFORMATION

Car Parking: At the ground
Coach Parking: At the ground
Nearest Railway Station: Inverurie
Nearest Bus Station: Inverurie
Club Shop: Limited supply of merchandise available

GROUND INFORMATION

Away Supporters' Entrances & Sections:
No usual segregation

ADMISSION INFO (2013/2014 PRICES)

Adult Standing: £8.00 **Adult Seating**: £9.00
Child/Senior Citizen Standing: £4.00
Child/Senior Citizen Seating: £5.00
Note: Under-14s are admitted free with a paying adult
Programme Price: No programme is produced

DISABLED INFORMATION

Wheelchairs: Accommodated in the Covered Enclosure
Helpers: Admitted
Prices: Free of charge for the disabled
Disabled Toilets: Available
Contact: 07500 664434

Travelling Supporters' Information:
Routes: From the North: Take the A96 to the Inverurie bypass then turn left at the Morrisons roundabout along Blackhall Road and left at the next roundabout into Boroughmuir Drive. Cross the next roundabout and then turn 1st right into Hawlaw Road for the ground; From the South: Take the A96 to the Inverurie bypass then as above.

KEITH FC

Founded: 1910
Nickname: 'Maroons'
Ground: Kynoch Park, Balloch Road, Keith AB55 5EN
Ground Capacity: 4,000
Seating Capacity: 370
Record Attendance: 5,820 (4th February 1928)
Pitch Size: 110 × 75 yards

Colours: Shirts and shorts are Maroon with Blue trim
Telephone N°: (01542) 882629
Fax Number: (01542) 882631
Contact Phone N°: (01542) 882629
Mobile Phone Contact N°: 07836 701779
Web Site: www.keithfc.co.uk
E-mail: keithfc@highlandleague.com

GENERAL INFORMATION

Car Parking: Street parking in Balloch Road, Moss Street and Reidhaven Square
Coach Parking: Balloch Road or Bridge Street Coach Park
Nearest Railway Station: Keith (1 mile)
Nearest Bus Station: Keith
Club Shop: At the ground
Opening Times: Wednesday to Friday 9.00am to 12.30pm
Telephone N°: (01542) 882629

GROUND INFORMATION

Away Supporters' Entrances & Sections:
No usual segregation except for some Cup Ties

ADMISSION INFO (2013/2014 PRICES)

Adult Standing: £7.00
Adult Seating: £8.00
Child Standing: £4.00
Child Seating: £5.00
Note: Under-14s are admitted free with a paying adult
Programme Price: £1.00

DISABLED INFORMATION

Wheelchairs: Accommodated
Helpers: Admitted
Prices: Free entry for the disabled
Disabled Toilets: Available

Travelling Supporters' Information:
Routes: From Inverness: Follow the A96 through Keith before turning left opposite the newsagents and public toilets in Reidhaven Square. Follow signs for the Moray College Learning Centre, take the next left into Balloch Road and the ground is on the right; From Aberdeen: After Entering Keith turn right opposite the newsagents in Reidhaven Square. Then as above.

LOSSIEMOUTH FC

Founded: 1945
Nickname: 'Coasters'
Ground: Grant Park, Kellas Avenue, Lossiemouth IV31 6JG
Ground Capacity: 2,400 **Seating Capacity**: 150
Record Attendance: 2,800 (28th December 1948)
Pitch Size: 110 × 67 yards
Colours: Red shirts and shorts

Telephone Nº: (01343) 813717
Fax Number: (01343) 813717
Social Club Nº: (01343) 813168
Contact Address: Alan McIntosh, 3 Forties Place, Lossiemouth IV31 6SS
Contact Phone Nº: (01343) 813328 & (07890) 749053
Contact e-mail: alanlfcsec@aol.com
Web Site: www.lossiemouthfc.co.uk

GENERAL INFORMATION

Car Parking: At the ground
Coach Parking: At the ground
Nearest Railway Station: Elgin
Nearest Bus Station: Lossiemouth
Club Shop: At the ground
Opening Times: Matchdays only
Telephone Nº: (01343) 813168

GROUND INFORMATION

Away Supporters' Entrances & Sections:
No usual segregation

ADMISSION INFO (2013/2014 PRICES)

Adult Standing: £7.00 **Adult Seating**: £8.00
Child Standing: £3.50
Child Seating: £4.50
Note: Under-14s are admitted free with a paying adult
Programme Price: £1.00

DISABLED INFORMATION

Wheelchairs: Accommodated
Helpers: Admitted
Prices: Free of charge for the disabled
Disabled Toilets: Available
Contact: (01343) 813328 (Alan McIntosh) (Please book)

Travelling Supporters' Information:
Routes: Take the A941 to Lossiemouth. As you enter the town take the 3rd turning on the right into Moray Street. Continue along Moray Street then take the 4th turning on the right into Kellas Avenue. Grant Park is at the end of this road.

NAIRN COUNTY FC

Founded: 1914
Nickname: 'The Wee County'
Ground: Station Park, Balblair Road, Nairn IV12 5LT
Ground Capacity: 1,700
Seating Capacity: 250
Record Attendance: 4,000 (2nd September 1950)
Pitch Size: 106 × 70 yards

Colours: Maize Yellow shirts with Black shorts
Telephone N°: (01667) 454298
Fax Number: (01667) 456354
Contact Address: Peter Mackintosh, c/o Club
Contact Phone N°: 07710 468436
Web Site: www.nairncountyfc.co.uk
E-mail: info@nairncountyfc.co.uk

GENERAL INFORMATION

Car Parking: Limited number of spaces adjoining the ground
Coach Parking: At the ground
Nearest Railway Station: Nairn (adjacent)
Nearest Bus Station: King Street, Nairn (½ mile)
Club Shop: At the ground
Opening Times: Matchdays only

GROUND INFORMATION

Away Supporters' Entrances & Sections:
No usual segregation

ADMISSION INFO (2013/2014 PRICES)

Adult Standing: £8.00
Adult Seating: £9.00
Senior Citizen/Child Standing: £5.00
Senior Citizen/Child Seating: £6.00
Note: Under-14s are admitted free with a paying adult
Programme Price: £1.50

DISABLED INFORMATION

Wheelchairs: Accommodated in the Stand
Helpers: Admitted
Prices: £5.00 for disabled fans
Disabled Toilets: Available
Contact: (01667) 454298 (Bookings are appreciated)

Travelling Supporters' Information:
Routes: The ground is situated on the south side of Nairn at Balblair Road, adjacent to the Railway Station.

ROTHES FC

Founded: 1938
Former Names: Rothes Victoria FC
Nickname: 'The Speysiders'
Ground: Mackessack Park, Station Street, Rothes, AB38 7BY
Ground Capacity: 2,700
Seating Capacity: 160
Record Attendance: 2,054 (September 1946)
Pitch Size: 108 × 74 yards

Colours: Tangerine shirts with Black shorts
Telephone Nº: 07821 192502 or 07827 774797 (Matchdays only)
Social Club Nº: (01340) 831348
Contact Address: Andrew Simpson, Arndilly View, 69 Land Street, Rothes AB38 7BB
Contact Phone Nº: (01340) 832314
Web site: www.spanglefish.com/rothesfootballclub
E-mail: rothesfc@highlandleague.com

GENERAL INFORMATION

Car Parking: At the ground
Coach Parking: At the ground
Nearest Railway Station: Elgin
Nearest Bus Station: Elgin
Club Shop: At the ground during home matches and also via the club's web site.

GROUND INFORMATION

Away Supporters' Entrances & Sections:
No usual segregation

ADMISSION INFO (2013/2014 PRICES)

Adult Standing: £8.00
Adult Seating: £9.00
Child Standing: £4.00
Child Seating: £5.00
Note: Under-14s are admitted free with a paying adult
Programme Price: £1.50

DISABLED INFORMATION

Wheelchairs: Accommodated
Helpers: Admitted
Prices: Normal prices apply
Disabled Toilets: Available

Travelling Supporters' Information:
Routes: From the A96 take the A941 signposted for Perth and follow into Rothes. After entering the town take the 2nd exit (A941 Perth) before immediately turning 1st left down a small track. Follow this past the distillery to reach the ground.

STRATHSPEY THISTLE FC

Founded: 1993
Former Names: None
Nickname: 'Thistle'
Ground: Seafield Park, Grantown-on-Spey
Ground Capacity: 1,500
Seating Capacity: 320
Pitch Size: 108 x 70 yards

Colours: Blue shirts with White shorts
Telephone Nº: None
Contact Address: Malky Taylor, Clunemore, Kinchurdy Road, Boat of Garten PH24 3BP
Contact Phone Nº: (01479) 831233
Web site: www.strathspeythistle.com
E-mail: strathspeythistlefc@highlandleague.com

GENERAL INFORMATION

Car Parking: At the ground and nearby
Coach Parking: At the ground
Nearest Railway Station: Aviemore (14 miles)
Club Shop: None

GROUND INFORMATION

Away Supporters' Entrances & Sections:
No usual segregation

ADMISSION INFO (2013/2014 PRICES)

Adult Standing: £8.00 **Adult Seating**: £8.00
Child Standing: £4.00
Child Seating: £4.00
Note: Under-14s are admitted free with a paying adult
Programme Price: £1.50

DISABLED INFORMATION

Wheelchairs: No special accommodation
Helpers: Admitted
Prices: Concessionary prices are charged for the disabled
Disabled Toilets: Available
Contact: (01479) 872277 (Bookings are not necessary)

Travelling Supporters' Information:
Routes: From Forres: Take the A939 to Grantown-on-Spey and upon entering town, take the 1st left then the 1st right into Heathfield Road. Continue along then turn 1st left into Golf Course Road and the ground is ¼ mile along the road.
From Aviemore: Take the A939 to Grantown-on-Spey and turn right at the first set of traffic lights into Woodside Avenue. Continue along the road for about ½ mile then turn right into Golf Course Road for the ground.

TURRIFF UNITED FC

Founded: 1954
Former Names: None
Nickname: 'Turra' or 'United'
Ground: The Haughs, Turriff AB53 4ER
Ground Capacity: 2,135
Seating Capacity: 320
Record Attendance: 500
Pitch Size: 106 x 70 yards

Colours: Navy Blue shirts and shorts
Telephone N°: (01888) 563486
Fax Number: (01888) 562909
Contact Address: Gairn Ritchie, 29 Slackadale Gardens, Turriff AB53 4UA
Contact Phone N°: (01888) 562904
Web site: www.turriffunited.co.uk

GENERAL INFORMATION

Car Parking: At the ground
Coach Parking: At the ground
Nearest Railway Station: Inverurie (20 miles)
Nearest Bus Station: Turriff
Club Shop: Available via the Club's web site only

GROUND INFORMATION

Away Supporters' Entrances & Sections:
No usual segregation

ADMISSION INFO (2013/2014 PRICES)

Adult Standing: £7.00
Adult Seating: £8.00
Child Standing: £4.00
Child Seating: £4.00
Note: Under-14s are admitted free with a paying adult
Programme Price: £1.50

DISABLED INFORMATION

Wheelchairs: Accommodated
Helpers: Admitted
Prices: Normal prices for the disabled and helpers
Disabled Toilets: Available
Contact: 07919 095322 (Bookings are necessary)

Travelling Supporters' Information:
Routes: From the North: Take the A947 to Turriff and, after the only roundabout in town, turn 1st right down to The Haughs. The ground is adjacent to the Swimming Pool.

WICK ACADEMY FC

Founded: 1893
Nickname: 'The Scorries'
Ground: Harmsworth Park, South Road, Wick, Caithness KW1 5NH
Ground Capacity: 2,000
Seating Capacity: 433
Record Attendance: 2,000 (30th July 1984)
Pitch Size: 106 × 76 yards

Colours: Black and White striped shirts, White shorts
Telephone Nº: (01955) 602446
Fax Number: (01955) 602446
Contact Address: Alan Farquher, 22 Wellington Street, Wick KW1 5HS
Contact Phone Nº: (01955) 604924
Web Site: www.wick-academy.co.uk

GENERAL INFORMATION

Car Parking: At the ground
Coach Parking: At the ground
Nearest Railway Station: Wick (10 minutes walk)
Nearest Bus Station: Wick
Club Shop: Wick Sports Shop, High Street, Wick
Opening Times: 9.00am to 5.00pm
Telephone Nº: (01955) 602930

GROUND INFORMATION

Away Supporters' Entrances & Sections:
No usual segregation

ADMISSION INFO (2013/2014 PRICES)

Adult Standing: £6.00
Adult Seating: £7.00
Child Standing: £3.00
Child Seating: £4.00
Note: Under-14s are admitted free with a paying adult
Programme Price: £1.00

DISABLED INFORMATION

Wheelchairs: 2 spaces available in the North Stand
Helpers: Please phone the club for details
Prices: Please phone the club for details
Disabled Toilets: None
Contact: (01955) 603883 (Bookings are not necessary)

Travelling Supporters' Information:
Routes: The ground is situated on the A99 road from Inverness beside the Cemetery.

Scottish Premier League 2012/2013 Season	Aberdeen	Celtic	Dundee	Dundee United	Hearts	Hibernian	Inverness C.T.	Kilmarnock	Motherwell	Ross County	St. Johnstone	St. Mirren
Aberdeen		0-2	2-0	2-2	0-0	2-1	2-3	0-2	3-3	0-0	2-0	0-0
			1-0		2-0	0-0		1-0	0-0	0-1		0-0
					1-1							
Celtic	1-0		2-0	4-0	1-0	2-2	0-1	0-2	1-0	4-0	1-1	2-0
	4-3		5-0	6-2	4-1	3-0	4-1	4-1			4-0	
Dundee	1-3	0-2		0-3	1-0	3-1	1-4	0-0	1-2	0-1	1-3	0-2
	1-1				1-0		1-1	2-3	0-3	0-2	2-2	2-1
Dundee United	1-1	2-2	3-0		0-3	3-0	4-4	3-3	1-2	0-0	1-1	3-4
	1-0	0-4	1-1		3-1	2-2			1-3	1-1	0-1	
Heart of Midlothian	2-0	0-4	0-1	2-1		0-0	2-2	1-3	1-0	2-2	2-0	1-0
			1-0			1-2	2-3	0-3	1-2	4-2	2-0	3-0
Hibernian	0-1	1-0	3-0	2-1	1-1		2-2	2-1	2-3	0-1	2-0	2-1
	0-0		1-1		0-0		1-2	2-2			1-3	3-3
			1-0									
Inverness Caledonian Thistle	1-1	2-4	4-1	4-0	1-1	3-0		1-1	1-5	3-1	1-1	2-2
	3-0	1-3		0-0				1-1	4-3	2-1	0-0	
				1-2								
Kilmarnock	1-3	1-3	0-0	3-1	1-0	1-1	1-2		1-2	3-0	1-2	3-1
	1-1		1-2	2-3	0-1	1-3			2-0			1-1
												1-3
Motherwell	4-1	0-2	1-1	0-1	0-0	0-4	4-1	2-2		3-2	1-1	1-1
		2-1		0-1		4-1	3-0			2-0	3-2	2-2
		3-1										
Ross County	2-1	1-1	1-1	1-2	2-2	3-2	0-0	0-0	0-0		1-2	0-0
		3-2		1-0		1-0	1-0	0-1	3-0		1-0	
		1-1										
St. Johnstone	1-2	2-1	1-0	0-0	2-2	0-1	0-0	2-1	1-3	1-1		2-1
	3-1	1-1		1-1			1-0	2-0	2-0	2-2		1-0
St. Mirren	1-4	0-5	3-1	0-1	2-0	1-2	2-2	1-1	2-1	5-4	1-1	
	0-0	1-1	1-2	0-0	2-0	0-1	2-1			1-4		

Scottish Premier League **Season 2012/2013**

Celtic	38	24	7	7	92	35	79
Motherwell	38	18	9	11	67	51	63
St. Johnstone	38	14	14	10	45	44	56
Inverness Caledonian Thistle	38	13	15	10	64	60	54
Ross County	38	13	14	11	47	48	53
Dundee United	38	11	14	13	51	62	47
Hibernian	38	13	12	13	49	52	51
Aberdeen	38	11	15	12	41	43	48
Kilmarnock	38	11	12	15	52	53	45
Heart of Midlothian	38	11	11	16	40	49	44
St. Mirren	38	9	14	15	47	60	41
Dundee	38	7	9	22	28	66	30

With 5 games of the season left, the Division was split into two groups of 6. The top half contended for the Championship while the bottom half decided relegation.

Teams in the bottom half at the time of the split may not overtake a team in the top 6 at the time of the split, hence the positioning of Hibernian and Aberdeen below Dundee United.

Scottish Football League Division One 2012/2013 Season	Airdrie United	Cowdenbeath	Dumbarton	Dunfermline Athletic	Falkirk	Greenock Morton	Hamilton Academical	Livingston	Partick Thistle	Raith Rovers
Airdrie United		0-3	4-1	1-2	1-4	2-3	0-4	1-3	1-1	0-0
		1-1	1-2	3-3	0-1	0-4	2-2	0-2	1-2	1-2
Cowdenbeath	1-1		0-1	0-4	1-1	3-4	1-0	1-1	0-3	4-4
	3-2		2-3	4-2	4-1	1-1	1-1	2-2	1-2	1-1
Dumbarton	3-4	0-3		0-2	1-2	1-5	3-3	3-4	2-0	4-2
	4-1	2-2		0-1	0-2	0-3	3-1	0-3	0-0	1-2
Dunfermline Athletic	1-3	3-0	4-0		0-1	2-2	1-1	4-0	0-1	3-1
	1-2	1-0	3-4		0-2	1-4	2-3	0-1	0-4	1-0
Falkirk	1-1	2-0	3-4	2-2		0-1	2-1	1-2	0-0	0-2
	4-3	4-0	1-3	1-0		4-1	0-2	2-0	0-2	1-1
Greenock Morton	2-0	1-0	3-0	4-2	1-2		0-1	2-2	3-1	1-0
	5-2	4-2	0-3	0-1	2-0		0-2	2-1	2-2	1-0
Hamilton Academical	3-0	2-1	2-1	0-3	1-1	1-1		1-2	1-0	0-1
	5-0	1-3	2-3	1-2	1-1	2-1		1-1	0-2	2-0
Livingston	0-2	1-1	5-0	2-1	2-1	2-2	0-0		1-2	2-1
	4-1	3-0	2-3	2-2	1-2	0-2	0-3		2-2	2-3
Partick Thistle	7-0	2-1	3-0	5-1	3-1	1-2	4-0	2-0		3-2
	1-0	2-1	3-0	3-3	4-1	1-0	1-0	6-1		0-0
Raith Rovers	2-0	2-2	2-2	1-3	2-1	3-3	2-0	0-0	1-1	
	2-0	0-1	3-2	1-1	0-0	2-1	0-2	0-2	0-0	

Scottish League Division One

Season 2012/2013

Partick Thistle	36	23	9	4	76	28	78
Greenock Morton	36	20	7	9	73	47	67
Falkirk	36	15	8	13	52	48	53
Livingston	36	14	10	12	58	56	52
Hamilton Academical	36	14	9	13	52	45	51
Raith Rovers	36	11	13	12	45	48	46
Dumbarton	36	13	4	19	58	83	43
Cowdenbeath	36	8	12	16	51	65	36
Dunfermline Athletic	36	14	7	15	62	59	34
Airdrie United	36	5	7	24	41	89	22

Dunfermline Athletic had 15 points deducted after entering administration.

Scottish Football League Division Two 2012/2013 Season	Albion Rovers	Alloa Athletic	Arbroath	Ayr United	Brechin City	East Fife	Forfar Athletic	Queen of the South	Stenhousemuir	Stranraer
Albion Rovers		0-3	4-0	2-0	1-2	0-3	2-3	0-3	4-4	2-1
		1-5	0-1	1-3	3-1	1-1	1-2	0-1	4-3	2-3
Alloa Athletic	5-1		2-3	1-0	2-2	1-1	2-1	1-0	0-2	3-0
	4-1		0-1	2-2	0-1	1-1	1-0	1-2	1-0	4-1
Arbroath	2-1	1-2		4-2	3-1	2-0	1-1	2-3	2-2	2-1
	2-1	0-1		1-4	0-1	1-0	3-1	1-1	0-0	1-0
Ayr United	2-1	0-0	2-0		3-0	2-3	2-3	2-4	1-1	2-1
	5-2	0-2	0-1		1-2	2-1	2-1	1-5	1-2	2-1
Brechin City	1-0	1-3	3-2	2-1		2-1	4-1	0-3	7-2	3-0
	2-0	3-2	2-0	2-1		6-0	3-4	0-6	1-2	2-2
East Fife	1-2	0-1	2-1	2-3	2-2		3-0	0-0	3-2	0-1
	2-0	2-1	0-1	3-3	0-3		1-2	2-3	1-2	1-1
Forfar Athletic	4-2	2-3	1-1	2-1	1-0	3-2		1-5	3-2	4-0
	4-2	0-1	2-4	2-1	1-4	3-2		0-4	3-3	3-1
Queen of the South	1-0	1-0	6-0	2-0	1-0	1-0	2-0		2-2	4-1
	3-0	0-0	5-1	2-0	2-1	2-2	3-1		2-1	2-0
Stenhousemuir	1-0	0-2	2-2	1-1	3-1	3-0	0-4	1-3		0-0
	0-1	1-1	1-0	4-0	3-3	2-1	2-0	2-1		1-2
Stranraer	1-1	3-2	1-1	2-0	0-2	2-6	4-1	0-2	1-1	
	3-2	1-2	2-0	0-1	3-2	3-1	0-3	0-5	1-1	

Scottish League Division Two

Season 2012/2013

Queen of the South	36	29	5	2	92	23	92
Alloa Athletic	36	20	7	9	62	35	67
Brechin City	36	19	4	13	72	59	61
Forfar Athletic	36	17	3	16	67	74	54
Arbroath	36	15	7	14	47	57	52
Stenhousemuir	36	12	13	11	59	59	49
Ayr United	36	12	5	19	53	65	41
Stranraer	36	10	7	19	43	71	37
East Fife	36	8	8	20	50	65	32
Albion Rovers	36	7	3	26	45	82	24

Scottish Football League Division Three 2012/2013 Season	Annan Athletic	Berwick Rangers	Clyde	East Stirlingshire	Elgin City	Montrose	Peterhead	Queen's Park	Rangers	Stirling Albion
Annan Athletic		3-2	1-3	5-2	2-0	2-1	2-1	2-3	0-0	5-2
		2-2	0-1	1-2	2-2	1-1	0-0	2-0	1-3	0-1
Berwick Rangers	3-1		2-1	3-0	0-0	1-4	1-1	2-0	1-1	4-1
	0-2		3-3	2-0	2-1	4-0	0-2	4-1	1-3	1-0
Clyde	2-1	2-1		2-1	2-2	1-2	0-2	0-3	0-2	2-1
	2-3	2-1		2-0	1-1	1-0	2-0	2-3	1-4	1-2
East Stirlingshire	2-2	0-1	3-0		1-4	2-2	2-1	0-2	2-6	3-1
	1-2	0-3	3-0		3-2	1-2	2-4	0-2	2-4	1-1
Elgin City	2-2	3-1	2-1	3-4		6-1	2-0	0-4	2-6	3-1
	3-1	1-2	4-2	3-2		3-2	0-3	3-5	0-1	1-2
Montrose	0-0	3-1	2-3	3-1	2-2		2-0	1-1	2-4	3-2
	5-1	1-3	1-1	2-2	4-1		0-6	1-2	0-0	2-2
Peterhead	2-0	1-0	1-0	2-0	1-1	2-0		1-0	2-2	2-2
	2-0	1-1	3-0	6-0	0-1	0-1		0-2	0-1	0-0
Queen's Park	2-2	1-1	1-0	1-2	1-1	2-2	0-0		0-1	2-1
	2-2	2-1	4-1	5-1	0-1	1-2	0-3		1-4	2-2
Rangers	3-0	4-2	3-0	5-1	5-1	4-1	2-0	2-0		2-0
	1-2	1-0	2-0	3-1	1-1	1-1	1-2	4-0		0-0
Stirling Albion	5-1	6-3	0-1	1-1	1-4	1-3	1-0	1-2	1-0	
	2-1	1-0	2-0	9-1	1-1	3-1	0-1	2-3	1-1	

Scottish League Division Three

Season 2012/2013

Rangers	36	25	8	3	87	29	83
Peterhead	36	17	8	11	52	28	59
Queen's Park	36	16	8	12	60	54	56
Berwick Rangers	36	14	7	15	59	55	49
Elgin City	36	13	10	13	67	69	49
Montrose	36	12	11	13	60	68	47
Stirling Albion	36	12	9	15	59	58	45
Annan Athletic	36	11	10	15	54	65	43
Clyde	36	12	4	20	42	66	40
East Stirlingshire	36	8	5	23	49	97	29

Highland Football League 2012/2013 Season	Brora Rangers	Buckie Thistle	Clachnacuddin	Cove Rangers	Deveronvale	Formartine United	Forres Mechanics	Fort William	Fraserburgh	Huntly	Inverurie Loco Works	Keith	Lossiemouth	Nairn County	Rothes	Strathspey Thistle	Turriff United	Wick Academy
Brora Rangers		1-3	1-2	1-1	4-1	1-2	0-1	12-2	0-3	1-0	2-1	4-1	6-0	3-4	2-0	3-0	4-0	5-0
Buckie Thistle	1-0		0-3	1-1	0-1	1-4	0-3	3-3	1-3	0-3	1-1	1-2	3-1	1-1	2-1	7-1	2-0	0-7
Clachnacuddin	1-0	2-3		0-1	1-2	1-3	3-1	4-0	1-4	3-1	3-3	1-1	3-2	1-0	3-1	5-0	1-2	1-0
Cove Rangers	2-2	2-1	3-2		3-1	2-1	3-1	6-0	4-1	1-0	7-0	2-2	4-0	3-1	5-0	9-0	7-0	3-1
Deveronvale	5-0	2-1	1-1	0-2		0-0	2-2	2-1	2-1	1-2	0-1	1-0	3-2	1-0	5-0	2-0	3-3	6-0
Formartine United	2-1	3-0	5-1	0-2	4-0		2-2	4-1	3-1	6-0	3-2	4-1	3-1	1-3	5-0	9-1	2-1	3-3
Forres Mechanics	1-2	3-2	1-3	0-2	2-2	2-1		5-0	1-1	1-1	2-3	1-1	5-2	0-1	8-1	6-1	1-2	4-1
Fort William	1-5	1-5	0-2	0-6	1-7	1-5	1-3		0-7	0-1	2-4	0-3	0-0	1-5	0-2	1-0	0-2	0-3
Fraserburgh	0-0	2-0	2-3	1-1	4-0	2-3	2-2	6-0		3-2	3-1	2-3	5-0	2-4	5-1	4-1	4-2	1-3
Huntly	1-1	0-1	1-2	0-3	0-3	1-6	0-1	3-0	2-1		4-4	1-3	3-1	3-2	7-0	7-1	2-1	2-3
Inverurie Loco Works	0-1	2-2	1-3	0-5	0-1	1-3	0-2	3-1	2-0	3-1		3-1	3-1	0-1	2-0	5-0	1-0	2-0
Keith	1-2	1-2	1-2	1-0	1-1	0-1	2-1	1-1	0-3	2-0	2-4		3-4	1-2	4-2	5-1	1-1	1-6
Lossiemouth	1-3	0-4	0-1	2-3	0-4	1-2	0-3	3-1	0-4	0-4	1-4	2-4		1-3	1-2	1-0	1-3	0-4
Nairn County	6-0	2-2	3-2	3-2	2-1	1-4	1-0	5-1	1-1	1-3	3-3	1-1	4-1		4-0	1-0	4-0	3-2
Rothes	1-9	2-3	1-2	0-2	1-1	0-7	0-3	5-0	0-2	0-5	1-9	0-3	3-2	1-3		0-1	2-2	0-4
Strathspey Thistle	1-5	1-3	0-3	0-2	0-3	0-3	2-4	1-0	0-1	2-3	0-3	0-1	3-1	0-3	3-1		0-2	1-4
Turriff United	4-2	1-1	1-2	2-1	2-1	2-1	2-5	2-0	0-1	7-3	3-0	4-1	3-0	0-2	7-1	1-2		4-3
Wick Academy	3-0	2-1	4-0	2-1	4-1	3-1	3-1	1-0	4-1	4-0	1-0	5-1	5-3	1-0	5-0	4-0	6-2	

Highland Football League

Season 2012/2013

Cove Rangers	34	25	5	4	101	26	80
Formartine United	34	25	3	6	106	39	78
Wick Academy	34	25	1	8	101	48	76
Nairn County	34	22	5	7	80	43	71
Clachnacuddin	34	21	3	10	68	49	66
Fraserburgh	34	18	5	11	83	47	59
Deveronvale	34	17	7	10	66	45	58
Brora Rangers	34	17	4	13	83	52	55
Forres Mechanics	34	16	7	11	78	49	55
Inverurie Loco Works	34	16	5	13	71	60	53
Turriff United	34	16	4	14	68	67	52
Buckie Thistle	34	13	7	14	58	62	46
Huntly	34	14	3	17	66	68	45
Keith	34	12	7	15	56	65	43
Strathspey Thistle	34	5	0	29	23	112	15
Rothes	34	4	2	28	29	126	14
Lossiemouth	34	3	1	30	35	108	10
Fort William	34	1	3	30	20	126	6

Scottish Cup 2012/2013

Round 1	25th Aug 2012	Threave Rovers	0	Vale of Leithen	1
Round 1	25th Aug 2012	Bonnyrigg Rose Athletic	2	Girvan	1
Round 1	25th Aug 2012	Huntly	2	Wigtown & Bladnoch	2
Round 1	25th Aug 2012	Shotts Bon Accord	1	Edinburgh City	1
Round 1	25th Aug 2012	Irvine Meadow	4	Gala Fairydean	0
Round 1	25th Aug 2012	Edinburgh University	1	St. Cuthbert Wanderers	2
Round 1	25th Aug 2012	Formartine United	3	Brora Rangers	2
Round 1	25th Aug 2012	Civil Service Strollers	4	Newton Stewart	0
Round 1	25th Aug 2012	Spartans	0	Wick Academy	2
Round 1	25th Aug 2012	Glasgow University	0	Selkirk	2
Round 1	25th Aug 2012	Clachnacuddin	2	Lossiemouth	1
Round 1	25th Aug 2012	Hawick Royal Albert	1	Golspie Sutherland	4
Round 1	25th Aug 2012	Fraserburgh	4	Coldstream	0
Round 1	25th Aug 2012	Whitehill Welfare	2	Inverurie Loco Works	4
Round 1	25th Aug 2012	Buckie Thistle	0	Rothes	0
Round 1	25th Aug 2012	Hermes	1	Deveronvale	4
Round 1	25th Aug 2012	Preston Athletic	0	Nairn County	2
Round 1	25th Aug 2012	Turriff United	6	Burntisland Shipyard	1
Replay	1st Sep 2012	Edinburgh City	4	Shotts Bon Accord	1
Replay	1st Sep 2012	Rothes	0	Buckie Thistle	4
Replay	1st Sep 2012	Wigtown & Bladnoch	0	Huntly	2
Round 2	29th Sep 2012	Cove Rangers	7	Golspie Sutherland	0
Round 2	29th Sep 2012	Fraserburgh	1	East Stirlingshire	2
Round 2	29th Sep 2012	Forres Mechanics	0	Rangers	1
Round 2	29th Sep 2012	Clachnacuddin	4	Formartine United	2
Round 2	29th Sep 2012	Civil Service Strollers	1	Turriff United	2
Round 2	29th Sep 2012	Montrose	1	Edinburgh City	3
Round 2	29th Sep 2012	Buckie Thistle	0	Annan Athletic	0
Round 2	29th Sep 2012	Berwick Rangers	1	Wick Academy	0
Round 2	29th Sep 2012	Selkirk	1	Vale of Leithen	1
Round 2	29th Sep 2012	Inverurie Loco Works	4	Huntly	3
Round 2	29th Sep 2012	Deveronvale	3	Peterhead	2
Round 2	29th Sep 2012	Elgin City	3	St. Cuthbert Wanderers	1
Round 2	29th Sep 2012	Dalbeattie Star	0	Stirling Albion	5
Round 2	29th Sep 2012	Queen's Park	3	Irvine Meadow	0
Round 2	29th Sep 2012	Stirling University	0	Bonnyrigg Rose	1
Round 2	29th Sep 2012	Clyde	3	Nairn County	3
Replay	6th Oct 2012	Annan Athletic	1	Buckie Thistle	2
Replay	6th Oct 2012	Vale of Leithen	5	Selkirk	1
Replay	6th Oct 2012	Nairn County	3	Clyde	2
Round 3	3rd Nov 2012	Rangers	7	Alloa Athletic	0
Round 3	3rd Nov 2012	Elgin City	5	East Fife	1
Round 3	3rd Nov 2012	Buckie Thistle	0	Turriff United	1
Round 3	3rd Nov 2012	Dumbarton	4	East Stirlingshire	1
Round 3	3rd Nov 2012	Airdrie United	2	Raith Rovers	2
Round 3	3rd Nov 2012	Stranraer	1	Queens Park	1
Round 3	3rd Nov 2012	Partick Thistle	2	Cove Rangers	1
Round 3	3rd Nov 2012	Forfar Athletic	3	Nairn County	3
Round 3	3rd Nov 2012	Albion Rovers	1	Greenock Morton	1

Round 3	3rd Nov 2012	Cowdenbeath	8	Vale of Leithen	1	
Round 3	3rd Nov 2012	Edinburgh City	0	Queen of the South	2	
Round 3	3rd Nov 2012	Stirling Albion	0	Deveronvale	1	
Round 3	3rd Nov 2012	Inverurie Loco Works	3	Arbroath	3	
Round 3	3rd Nov 2012	Ayr United	2	Clachnacuddin	1	
Round 3	3rd Nov 2012	Stenhousemuir	1	Berwick Rangers	1	
Round 3	3rd Nov 2012	Brechin City	2	Bonnyrigg Rose	2	
Replay	10th Nov 2012	Bonnyrigg Rose Athletic	0	Brechin City	6	
Replay	10th Nov 2012	Queens Park	0	Stranraer	4	
Replay	10th Nov 2012	Nairn County	2	Forfar Athletic	3	
Replay	10th Nov 2012	Arbroath	3	Inverurie Loco Works	1	
Replay	13th Nov 2012	Greenock Morton	3	Albion Rovers	0	
Replay	13th Nov 2012	Berwick Rangers	2	Stenhousemuir	5	
Replay	13th Nov 2012	Raith Rovers	4	Airdrie United	3	(aet)
Round 4	1st Dec 2012	Ross County	3	Inverness Caledonian Thistle	3	
Round 4	1st Dec 2012	Aberdeen	1	Motherwell	1	
Round 4	1st Dec 2012	Partick Thistle	0	Dunfermline Athletic	1	
Round 4	1st Dec 2012	Kilmarnock	2	Queen of the South	1	
Round 4	1st Dec 2012	Raith Rovers	2	Deveronvale	1	
Round 4	1st Dec 2012	Turriff United	1	Greenock Morton	1	
Round 4	1st Dec 2012	Livingston	0	Dundee	2	
Round 4	1st Dec 2012	Forfar Athletic	2	Ayr United	1	
Round 4	1st Dec 2012	Celtic	1	Arbroath	1	
Round 4	1st Dec 2012	Stranraer	0	Dundee United	5	
Round 4	1st Dec 2012	Stenhousemuir	0	Falkirk	1	
Round 4	1st Dec 2012	St. Mirren	2		0	
Round 4	2nd Dec 2012	Rangers	3	Elgin City	0	
Round 4	2nd Dec 2012	Hibernian	1	Heart of Midlothian	0	
Round 4	17th Dec 2012	Dumbarton	1	Hamilton Academical	3	
Round 4	17th Dec 2012	Cowdenbeath	0	St. Johnstone	3	
Replay	11th Dec 2012	Motherwell	1	Aberdeen	2	
Replay	11th Dec 2012	Inverness Caledonian Thistle	2	Ross County	1	
Replay	12th Dec 2012	Arbroath	0	Celtic	1	
Replay	17th Dec 2012	Greenock Morton	6	Turriff United	0	
Round 5	2nd Feb 2013	Dundee United	3	Rangers	0	
Round 5	2nd Feb 2013	St. Mirren	2	St. Johnstone	0	
Round 5	2nd Feb 2013	Dunfermline Athletic	0	Hamilton Academical	2	
Round 5	2nd Feb 2013	Falkirk	4	Forfar Athletic	1	
Round 5	2nd Feb 2013	Kilmarnock	2	Inverness Caledonian Thistle	0	
Round 5	3rd Feb 2013	Raith Rovers	0	Celtic	3	
Round 5	3rd Feb 2013	Dundee	5	Greenock Morton	1	
Round 5	3rd Feb 2013	Hibernian	1	Aberdeen	0	
Quarter-final	2nd Mar 2013	St. Mirren	1	Celtic	2	
Quarter-final	2nd Mar 2013	Hamilton Academical	1	Falkirk	2	
Quarter-final	3rd Mar 2013	Dundee	1	Dundee United	2	
Quarter-final	3rd Mar 2013	Kilmarnock	2	Hibernian	4	
Semi-final	13th Apr 2013	Hibernian	4	Falkirk	3	(aet)
Semi-final	14th Apr 2013	Dundee United	3	Celtic	4	(aet)
FINAL	26th May 2013	Hibernian	0	Celtic	3	

Scottish League Challenge Cup 2012/2013

Round 1	28th Jul 2012	Annan Athletic	1	Livingston	0	
Round 1	28th Jul 2012	Berwick Rangers	2	Queen's Park	2	(aet)
		Queen's Park won 3-2 on penalties.				
Round 1	28th Jul 2012	Clyde	0	Partick Thistle	1	
Round 1	28th Jul 2012	Cowdenbeath	1	Alloa Athletic	1	(aet)
		Cowdenbeath won 3-1 on penalties.				
Round 1	28th Jul 2012	Dumbarton	0	Queen of the South	1	
Round 1	28th Jul 2012	East Stirlingshire	3	Ayr United	1	
Round 1	28th Jul 2012	Elgin City	5	Arbroath	7	
Round 1	28th Jul 2012	Falkirk	3	Stirling Albion	0	
Round 1	28th Jul 2012	Forfar Athletic	3	Dunfermline Athletic	2	
Round 1	28th Jul 2012	Greenock Morton	2	Albion Rovers	0	
Round 1	28th Jul 2012	Hamilton Academical	0	Airdrie United	1	
Round 1	28th Jul 2012	Montrose	4	Inverurie Locos	2	
Round 1	28th Jul 2012	Peterhead	1	East Fife	2	
Round 1	28th Jul 2012	Stranraer	1	Stenhousemuir	2	
Round 1	28th Jul 2012	Wick Academy	2	Raith Rovers	4	
Round 1	29th Jul 2012	Brechin City	1	Rangers	2	(aet)
Round 2	14th Aug 2012	Annan Athletic	0	Stenhousemuir	3	
Round 2	14th Aug 2012	Arbroath	3	Forfar Athletic	2	
Round 2	14th Aug 2012	Cowdenbeath	3	East Fife	0	
Round 2	14th Aug 2012	East Stirlingshire	3	Airdrie United	0	
Round 2	14th Aug 2012	Greenock Morton	1	Queen of the South	2	(aet)
Round 2	14th Aug 2012	Queen's Park	4	Partick Thistle	5	
Round 2	14th Aug 2012	Raith Rovers	5	Montrose	2	
Round 2	21st Aug 2012	Falkirk	0	Rangers	1	
Quarter-Fina	9th Sep 2012	Arbroath	1	Stenhousemuir	0	
Quarter-Fina	9th Sep 2012	East Stirlingshire	1	Cowdenbeath	2	
Quarter-Fina	9th Sep 2012	Partick Thistle	3	Raith Rovers	0	
Quarter-Fina	18th Sep 2012	Rangers	2	Queen of the South	2	(aet)
		Queen of the South won 4-3 on penalties.				
Semi-final	14th Oct 2012	Cowdenbeath	0	Partick Thistle	1	
Semi-final	14th Oct 2012	Queen of the South	2	Arbroath	1	(aet)
FINAL	7th Apr 2013	Partick Thistle	1	Queen of the South	1	(aet)
		Queen of the South won 6-5 on penalties.				

Scottish League Cup 2012/2013

Round 1	31st Jul 2012	Peterhead	0	Dundee	0	(aet)
		Dundee won 4-1 on penalties				
Round 1	4th Aug 2012	Queen of the South	5	Alloa Athletic	2	
Round 1	4th Aug 2012	Stranraer	0	Livingston	8	
Round 1	4th Aug 2012	Raith Rovers	4	Berwick Rangers	3	
Round 1	4th Aug 2012	Stenhousemuir	4	Brechin City	0	
Round 1	4th Aug 2012	Montrose	2	Cowdenbeath	1	
Round 1	4th Aug 2012	Ayr United	6	Clyde	1	
Round 1	4th Aug 2012	Queen's Park	3	Airdrie United	2	(aet)
Round 1	4th Aug 2012	Dumbarton	2	Albion Rovers	0	
Round 1	4th Aug 2012	Forfar Athletic	0	Partick Thistle	2	
Round 1	4th Aug 2012	Falkirk	2	Elgin City	0	
Round 1	4th Aug 2012	Hamilton Academical	2	Annan Athletic	0	
Round 1	4th Aug 2012	Arbroath	1	Stirling Albion	1	(aet)
		Arbroath won 3-2 on penalties				
Round 1	5th Aug 2012	East Stirlingshire	1	Greenock Morton	5	
Round 1	7th Aug 2012	Rangers	4	East Fife	0	
Round 2	22nd Aug 2012	Greenock Morton	0	Aberdeen	2	(aet)
Round 2	28th Aug 2012	Dunfermline Athletic	3	Montrose	0	
Round 2	28th Aug 2012	Hamilton Academical	1	Partick Thistle	0	(aet)
Round 2	28th Aug 2012	Kilmarnock	1	Stenhousemuir	2	
Round 2	28th Aug 2012	Livingston	3	Dumbarton	2	(aet)
Round 2	28th Aug 2012	Ross County	1	Raith Rovers	4	
Round 2	28th Aug 2012	Queen of the South	2	Hibernian	0	
Round 2	29th Aug 2012	Arbroath	0	Inverness Caledonian Thistle	2	
Round 2	29th Aug 2012	St. Mirren	5	Ayr United	1	
Round 2	29th Aug 2012	Queen's Park	2	Dundee	1	
Round 2	30th Aug 2012	Rangers	3	Falkirk	0	
Round 3	25th Sep 2012	Celtic	4	Raith Rovers	1	
Round 3	25th Sep 2012	Heart of Midlothian	3	Livingston	1	
Round 3	25th Sep 2012	Queen of the South	0	Dundee United	1	
Round 3	25th Sep 2012	St. Johnstone	4	Queen's Park	1	
Round 3	25th Sep 2012	St. Mirren	1	Hamilton Academical	0	
Round 3	25th Sep 2012	Stenhousemuir	1	Inverness Caledonian Thistle	1	(aet)
		Inverness Caledonian Thistle won 6-5 on penalties				
Round 3	26th Sep 2012	Rangers	2	Motherwell	0	
Round 3	26th Sep 2012	Dunfermline Athletic	0	Aberdeen	1	
Quarter-final	30th Oct 2012	Aberdeen	2	St. Mirren	2	(aet)
		St. Mirren won 4-2 on penalties				
Quarter-final	30th Oct 2012	Celtic	5	St. Johnstone	0	
Quarter-final	31st Oct 2012	Dundee United	1	Heart of Midlothian	1	(aet)
		Heart of Midlothian won 5-4 on penalties				
Quarter-final	31st Oct 2012	Rangers	0	Inverness Caledonian Thistle	3	
Semi-final	26th Jan 2013	Inverness Caledonian Thistle	1	Heart of Midlothian	1	(aet)
		Heart of Midlothian won 5-4 on penalties				
Semi-final	27th Jan 2013	St. Mirren	3	Celtic	2	
FINAL	17th Mar 2013	St. Mirren	3	Heart of Midlothian	2	

SCOTLAND INTERNATIONAL LINE-UPS AND STATISTICS 2009

28th March 2009
v NETHERLANDS (WCQ)
Amsterdam

McGregor	Rangers
Alexander	Burnley (sub. Hutton 73)
Berra	Wolverhampton Wanderers
Caldwell	Celtic
Naysmith	Sheffield United
Brown	Celtic
D. Fletcher	Manchester United
Ferguson	Rangers
McCormack	Cardiff City
Teale	Derby County (sub. Morrison 85)
K. Miller	Rangers (sub. S. Fletcher 71)

Result 0-3

1st April 2009
v ICELAND (WCQ) *Hampden Park*

Gordon	Sunderland
Hutton	Tottenham Hotspur
McManus	Celtic
Caldwell	Celtic
Naysmith	Sheffield United
Morrison	West Bromwich Albion (sub. Rae 90)
D. Fletcher	Manchester United
Brown	Celtic
McCormack	Cardiff City
K. Miller	Rangers
S. Fletcher	Hibernian (sub. Teale 78)

Result 2-1 McCormack, S. Fletcher

12th August 2009
v NORWAY (WCQ) *Oslo*

Marshall	Cardiff City
Hutton	Tottenham Hotspur
Davidson	Preston North End
S. Caldwell	Burnley (sub. McFadden 48)
G. Caldwell	Celtic
Alexander	Burnley
D. Fletcher	Manchester United
Commons	Derby County
Brown	Celtic
K. Miller	Rangers
McCormack	Cardiff City (sub. Berra 37 (sub. Whittaker 78))

Result 0-4

5th September 2009
MACEDONIA (WCQ) *Hampden Park*

Gordon	Sunderland
Hutton	Tottenham Hotspur
McManus	Celtic
Weir	Rangers
Davidson	Cardiff City (sub. Whittaker 14)
D. Fletcher	Manchester United
Alexander	Burnley
Brown	Celtic (sub. Hartley 73)
K. Miller	Rangers
S. Fletcher	Burnley (sub. Maloney 68)
McFadden	Birmingham City

Result 2-0 Brown, McFadden

9th September 2009
v NETHERLANDS (WCQ)
Hampden Park

Marshall	Cardiff City
Hutton	Tottenham Hotspur
Weir	Rangers
McManus	Celtic
Whittaker	Rangers
Hartley	Bristol City (sub. Commons 67)
Naismith	Rangers
Brown	Celtic
D. Fletcher	Manchester United
Maloney	Celtic (sub. O'Connor 83)
K. Miller	Rangers

Result 0-1

10th October 2009
v JAPAN *Yokohama*

Gordon	Sunderland
Berra	Wolverhampton Wanderers
G. Caldwell	Celtic
McManus	Celtic
Whittaker	Rangers
L. Wallace	Heart of Midlothian
Adam	Blackpool
Dorrans	West Bromwich Albion
R. Wallace	Preston North End
Conway	Dundee United
L. Miller	Aberdeen

Result 0-2

SCOTLAND INTERNATIONAL LINE-UPS AND STATISTICS 2009-2010

14th November 2009

v WALES *Cardiff*

Marshall	Cardiff City
Hutton	Tottenham Hotspur
McManus	Celtic
G. Caldwell	Celtic
Fox	Celtic (sub. S. Fletcher 55)
Dorrans	West Brom. Albion (sub. Robson 71)
D. Fletcher	Manchester United
Cowie	Watford (sub. Riordan 78)
K. Miller	Rangers (sub. L. Wallace 55)
Naismith	Rangers (sub. McCormack 62)
McFadden	Birmingham City (sub. Kyle 62)

Result 0-3

3rd March 2010

v CZECH REPUBLIC

Hampden Park

Gordon	Sunderland
Webster	Rangers (sub. Berra 46)
G. Caldwell	Wigan Athletic
Hutton	Tottenham Hotspur
L. Wallace	Heart of Midlothian
Robson	Middlesbrough (sub. Adam 69)
D. Fletcher	Manchester Utd. (sub. Whittaker 83)
Brown	Celtic
Thomson	Rangers (sub. Hartley 46)
Dorrans	West Bromwich Albion
K. Miller	Rangers (sub. Boyd 63)

Result 1-0 Brown

11th August 2010

v SWEDEN *Solna*

McGregor	Rangers
Broadfoot	Rangers (sub. Whittaker 74)
Wallace	Heart of Midlothian
Kenneth	Dundee United
Berra	Wolverhampton Wanderers
Robson	Middlesbrough (sub. Iwelumo 78)
D. Fletcher	Manchester United
K. Thomson	Middlesbrough (sub. Robertson 54)
S. Fletcher	Wolves (sub. Boyd 64)
C. Adam	Blackpool (sub. Morrison 64)
McFadden	Birmingham City

Result 0-3

3rd September 2010

v LITHUANIA (ECQ) *Kaunas*

McGregor	Rangers
Hutton	Tottenham Hotspur
Whittaker	Rangers (sub. Berra 90)
McManus	Middlesbrough
Weir	Rangers
McCulloch	Rangers
D. Fletcher	Manchester United
Robson	Middlesbrough (sub. McFadden 69)
Miller	Rangers
Brown	Celtic (sub. Morrison 76)
Naismith	Rangers

Result 0-0

7th September 2010

v LIECHTENSTEIN (ECQ)

Hampden Park

McGregor	Rangers
Hutton	Tottenham Hotspur
Wallace	Heart of Midlothian (sub. Robson 54)
McManus	Middlesbrough
Weir	Rangers
McCulloch	Rangers
D. Fletcher	Wolverhampton Wanderers
Brown	Celtic
Miller	Rangers
Boyd	Middlesbrough (sub. Naismith 66)
McFadden	Birmingham City (sub. Morrison 46)

Result 2-1 Miller, McManus

8th October 2010

v CZECH REPUBLIC (ECQ)

Prague

McGregor	Rangers
Hutton	Tottenham Hotspur
Whittaker	Rangers
McManus	Middlesbrough
Weir	Rangers
G. Caldwell	Wigan Athletic (sub. Miller 76)
D. Fletcher	Manchester United
Mackie	Queens Park Rangers (sub. Iwelumo 76)
Naismith	Rangers
Morrison	West Bromwich Albion (sub. Robson 84)
Dorrans	West Bromwich Albion

Result 0-1

SCOTLAND INTERNATIONAL LINE-UPS AND STATISTICS 2010-2011

12th October 2010

v SPAIN (ECQ) *Hampden Park*

McGregor	Rangers
Bardsley	Sunderland
Whittaker	Rangers
McManus	Middlesbrough
Weir	Rangers
McCulloch	Rangers (sub. Adam 46)
D. Fletcher	Manchester United
Morrison	West Brom. Albion (sub. Maloney 88)
Miller	Rangers
Naismith	Rangers
Dorrans	West Brom. Albion (sub. Mackie 80)

Result 2-3 Naismith, Pique (own goal)

16th November 2010

v FAROE ISLANDS *Aberdeen*

Gordon	Sunderland (sub. Bell 68)
Bardsley	Sunderland (sub. Saunders 71)
Crainey	Blackpool
S. Caldwell	Wigan Athletic
Wilson	Liverpool (sub. Kenneth 60)
Adam	Blackpool (sub. McArthur 55)
D. Fletcher	Manchester United (sub. Bryson 68)
Bannan	Aston Villa
Mackie	Queens Park Rangers
Commons	Derby County (sub. Goodwillie 76)
Maloney	Celtic

Result 3-0 Wilson, Commons, Mackie

9th February 2011

v NORTHERN IRELAND *Dublin*

McGregor	Rangers
Hutton	Tottenham Hotspur
Bardsley	Sunderland (sub. Wilson 56)
Berra	Wolverhampton Wanderers
S. Caldwell	Wigan Athletic
Adam	Blackpool (sub. Bannan 56)
Morrison	West Brom. Albion (sub. Maguire 78)
Naismith	Rangers (sub. Snodgrass 56)
Miller	Bursaspor (sub. Wilson 89)
McArthur	Wigan Athletic
Commons	Celtic (sub. Conway 71)

Result 3-0 Miller, McArthur, Commons

27th March 2011

v BRAZIL *Emirates Stadium, London*

McGregor	Rangers
Hutton	Tottenham Hotspur
Crainey	Blackpool
Berra	Wolves (sub. Wilson 73)
G. Caldwell	Wigan Athletic
Whittaker	Rangers (sub. Commons 64)
Adam	Blackpool (sub. Snodgrass 78)
Brown	Celtic
Miller	Bursaspor (sub. Mackail-Smith 87)
Morrison	West Brom. Albion (sub. Cowie 90)
McArthur	Wigan Athletic (sub. Bannan 56)

Result 0-2

25th May 2011

v WALES *Dublin*

McGregor	Rangers
Whittaker	Rangers (sub. Bardsley 81)
Crainey	Blackpool (sub. Martin 81)
Berra	Wolverhampton Wanderers
G. Caldwell	Wigan Athletic (sub. Hanley 84)
Morrison	West Brom. Albion (sub. Robson 73)
McCormack	Leeds United (sub. Bannan 73)
Brown	Celtic
Miller	Bursaspor
Adam	Blackpool (sub. McArthur 88)
Naismith	Rangers

Result 3-1 Morrison, Miller, Berra

29th May 2011

v REPUBLIC OF IRELAND *Dublin*

McGregor	Rangers
Whittaker	Rangers
Bardsley	Sunderland
Berra	Wolverhampton Wanderers
Hanley	Blackburn Rovers
Robson	Middlesbrough (sub. Maguire 75)
Forrest	Celtic (sub. McCormack 85)
Brown	Celtic
Miller	Bursaspor
Adam	Blackpool (sub. Bannan 62)
Naismith	Rangers

Result 0-1

SCOTLAND INTERNATIONAL LINE-UPS AND STATISTICS 2011

10th August 2011

v DENMARK *Hampden Park*

A. McGregor	Rangers
G. Caldwell	Wigan Athletic
P. Bardsley	Sunderland
S. Crainey	Blackpool
D. Wilson	Blackpool
C. Adam	Liverpool (sub. G. Dorrans 58)
S. Brown	Celtic (sub. D. Cowie 19)
J. Morrison	West Brom. Alb. (sub. B. Bannan 67)
R. Snodgrass	Leeds United (sub. G. Hanley 88)
K. Miller	Cardiff C. (sub. C. Mackail-Smith 57)
S. Naismith	Rangers (sub. J. Forrest 74)

Result 2-1 Kvist (og), Snodgrass

3rd September 2011

v CZECH REPUBLIC (EC)

Hampden Park

A. McGregor	Rangers
A. Hutton	Aston Villa
P. Bardsley	Sunderland (sub. D. Wilson 76)
C. Berra	Wolverhampton Wanderers
G. Caldwell	Wigan Athletic
C. Adam	Liverpool (sub. D. Cowie 79)
D. Fletcher	Manchester United
S. Brown	Celtic
K. Miller	Cardiff City
J. Morrison	West Bromwich Albion
S. Naismith	Rangers (sub. B. Robson 86)

Result 2-2 Miller, Fletcher

6th September 2011

v LITHUANIA (EC) *Hampden Park*

A. McGregor	Rangers
S. Whittaker	Rangers
P. Bardsley	Sunderland (sub. S. Crainey 70)
C. Berra	Wolverhampton Wanderers
G. Caldwell	Wigan Athletic
D. Cowie	Cardiff City
D. Fletcher	Manchester United
B. Bannan	Aston Villa (sub. R. Snodgrass 84)
D. Goodwillie	Blackburn Rovers
J. Morrison	West Brom. Alb. (sub. G. Dorrans 79)
S. Naismith	Rangers

Result 1-0 Naismith

8th October 2011

v LIECHTENSTEIN (EC) *Vaduz*

A. McGregor	Rangers
A. Hutton	Aston Villa
P. Bardsley	Sunderland
C. Berra	Wolverhampton Wanderers
G. Caldwell	Wigan Athletic
C. Adam	Liverpool
D. Fletcher	Manchester United
B. Bannan	Aston Villa
C. Mackail-Smith	Brighton & Hove Albion
J. Morrison	West Bromwich Albion
S. Naismith	Rangers

Result 1-0 Mackail-Smith

11th October 2011

v SPAIN (EC) *Alicante*

A. McGregor	Rangers
A. Hutton	Aston Villa
P. Bardsley	Sunderland
C. Berra	Wolverhampton Wanderers
G. Caldwell	Wigan Athletic
C. Adam	Liverpool (sub. J. Forrest 63)
D. Fletcher	Manchester United
J. Morrison	West Bromwich Albion
C. Mackail-Smith	Brighton & Hove Albion
B. Bannan	Aston Villa (sub. D. Goodwillie 63)
S. Naismith	Rangers

Result 1-3 Goodwillie (pen)

11th November 2011

v CYPRUS *Larnaca*

A. McGregor	Rangers
G. Caldwell	Wigan Athletic
C. Berra	Wolverhampton Wanderers
S. Whittaker	Rangers
P. Bardsley	Sunderland
B. Robson	Middlesbrough
J. Morrison	West Bromwich Albion
D. Fletcher	Manchester U. (sub. J. McArthur 63)
D. Cowie	Cardiff City
K. Miller	Cardiff C. (sub. C. Mackail-Smith 63)
J. Mackie	Queen's Park Rangers

Result 2-1 Miller, Mackie

SCOTLAND INTERNATIONAL LINE-UPS AND STATISTICS 2012

29th February 2012

v SLOVENIA *Koper*

A. McGregor Rangers
G. Caldwell Wigan Athletic
C. Berra Wolverhampton Wanderers
C. Mulgrew Celtic
R. Martin Norwich City
C. Adam Liverpool (sub. B. Bannan 46)
J. Morrison West Brom. Alb. (sub. G. Dorrans 72)
J. McArthur Wigan Athletic
J. Forrest Celtic (sub. B. Robson 87)
J. Mackie Q.P.R. (sub. K. Miller 81)
C. Mackail-Smith Brighton & Hove Albion (sub. R. Snodgrass 61)

Result 1-1 Berra

27th May 2012

v U.S.A. *Jacksonville*

A. McGregor Rangers
G. Caldwell Wigan Athletic
A. Webster Heart of Midlothian (sub. C. Berra 82)
P. Bardsley Sunderland (sub. S. Whittaker 59)
C. Mulgrew Celtic (sub. L. Wallace 68)
S. Brown Celtic
J. McArthur Wigan Athletic (sub. R. Martin 59)
B. Bannan Aston Villa (sub. D. Cowie 51)
M. Phillips Blackpool
S. Maloney Wigan Ath. (sub. C. Mackail-Smith 83)
K. Miller Cardiff City

Result 1-5 Cameron (og)

15th August 2012

v AUSTRALIA *Easter Road, Edinburgh*

A. McGregor Rangers (sub. M. Gilks 22)
A. Hutton Aston Villa (sub. R. Martin 67)
A. Webster Heart of Midlothian
C. Berra Wolverhampton Wanderers
D. Fox Southampton (sub. C. Mulgrew 69)
G. Caldwell Wigan Athletic (sub. I. Black 87)
R. Snodgrass Norwich City
J. Morrison West Brom. Alb. (sub. S. Maloney 27)
C. Adam Liverpool
S. Naismith Everton
J. Rhodes Huddersfield T. (sub. R. McCormack 67)

Result 3-1 Rhodes, Davidson (og), McCormack

8th September 2012

v SERBIA (WCQ) *Hampden Park*

A. McGregor Rangers
A. Hutton Aston Villa
A. Webster Heart of Midlothian
C. Berra Wolverhampton Wanderers
P. Dixon Huddersfield Town
G. Caldwell Wigan Athletic
R. Snodgrass Norwich City (sub. J. Forrest 69)
J. Morrison West Brom. Alb. (sub. J. Mackie 81)
C. Adam Stoke City
S. Naismith Everton
K. Miller Vancouver Whitecaps (sub. J. Rhodes 81)

Result 0-0

11th September 2012

v MACEDONIA (WCQ) *Hampden*

A. McGregor Rangers
A. Hutton Aston Villa
A. Webster Heart of Midlothian
C. Berra Wolverhampton Wanderers
P. Dixon Huddersfield Town
G. Caldwell Wigan Athletic
J. Forrest Celtic
J. Morrison West Brom Albion (sub. J. Rhodes 65)
S. Maloney Wigan Athletic
J. Mackie Q.P.R. (sub. S. Naismith 76)
K. Miller Vancouver Whitec. (sub. C. Adam 57)

Result 1-1 Miller

12th October 2012

v WALES (WCQ) *Cardiff*

A. McGregor Rangers
A. Hutton Aston Villa
G. Caldwell Wigan Athletic
C. Berra Wolverhampton Wanderers
D. Fox Southampton
J. Morrison West Brom. Albion (sub. K. Miller 84)
D. Fletcher Manchester United
S. Brown Celtic (sub.C. Adam 46)
S. Maloney Wigan Athletic
S. Fletcher Sunderland
K. Commons Celtic (sub. J. Mackie 84)

Result 1-2 Morrison

SCOTLAND INTERNATIONAL LINE-UPS AND STATISTICS 2012-2013

16th October 2012

v BELGIUM (WCQ) *Brussels*

A. McGregor — Rangers
A. Hutton — Aston Villa
G. Caldwell — Wigan Athletic
C. Berra — Wolverhampton Wanderers
D. Fox — Southampton
D. Fletcher — Manchester United
J. McArthur — Wigan Athletic
J. Morrison — West Brom. Alb. (sub. M. Phillips 80)
K. Commons — Celtic (sub J. Mackie 46)
S. Maloney — Wigan Athletic
S. Fletcher — Sunderland (sub. K. Miller 76)

Result 0-2

14th November 2012

v LUXEMBOURG *Luxembourg*

M. Gilks — Blackpool
S. Whittaker — Norwich City
G. Hanley — Blackburn Rovers
C. Berra — Wolverhampton Wanderers
P. Dixon — Southampton
C. Mulgrew — Celtic (sub. L. Kelly 46)
D. Fletcher — Manchester United
A. Shinnie — Inverness C.T. (sub. L. Griffiths 69)
S. Naismith — Everton
J. Rhodes — Blackburn Rov. (sub. M Davidson 90)
K. Miller — Vancouver Whitecaps

Result 2-1 Rhodes 2

6th February 2013

v ESTONIA *Pittodrie, Aberdeen*

A. McGregor — Rangers
A. Hutton — Mallorca
A. Webster — Heart of Midlothian
C. Berra — Wolverhampton Wanderers
C. Mulgrew — Celtic
S. Maloney — Wigan Athletic (sub. J. Rhodes 46)
S. Brown — Celtic (sub. J. Morrison 62)
C. Adam — Stoke City (sub. J. McArthur 61)
C. Burke — Birmingham C. (sub. R. Snodgrass 46)
S. Naismith — Everton (sub. K. Commons 75)
S. Fletcher — Sunderland (sub. K. Miller 67)

Result 1-0 Mulgrew

22nd March 2013

v WALES (WCQ) *Hampden Park*

A. McGregor — Rangers
A. Hutton — Mallorca
G. Caldwell — Wigan Athletic
G. Hanley — Blackburn Rovers
C. Mulgrew — Celtic
C. Burke — Birmingham City (sub. J. Rhodes 86)
J. McArthur — Wigan Athletic
G. Dorrans — West Brom. Albion (sub. C. Adam 63)
R. Snodgrass — Norwich City
S. Maloney — Wigan Athletic
S. Fletcher — Sunderland (sub. K. Miller 3)

Result 1-2 Hanley

26th March 2013

v SERBIA (WCQ) *Novi Sad*

D. Marshall — Cardiff City
A. Hutton — Mallorca
G. Hanley — Blackburn Rovers
G. Caldwell — Wigan Athletic
S. Whittaker — Norwich City
L. Bridcutt — Brighton & Hove Albion
J. McArthur — Wigan Athletic (sub. C. Adam 46)
G. Boyd — Hull City
S. Maloney — Wigan Athletic (sub. C. Burke 79)
S. Naismith — Everton
J. Rhodes — Blackburn Rovers (sub. K. Miller 79)

Result 0-2

7th June 2013

v CROATIA (WCQ) *Zagreb*

A. McGregor — Rangers
A. Hutton — Aston Villa
S. Whittaker — Norwich City
G. Hanley — Blackburn Rovers
R. Martin — Norwich City
S. Maloney — Wigan Athletic (sub. C. Conway 75)
J. Morrison — West Bromwich Albion
J. McArthur — Wigan Athletic
R. Snodgrass — Norwich City
B. Bannan — Aston Villa (sub. S. Naismith 63)
L. Griffiths — Hibernian (sub. J. Rhodes 64)

Result 1-0 Snodgrass

The Supporters' Guides Series

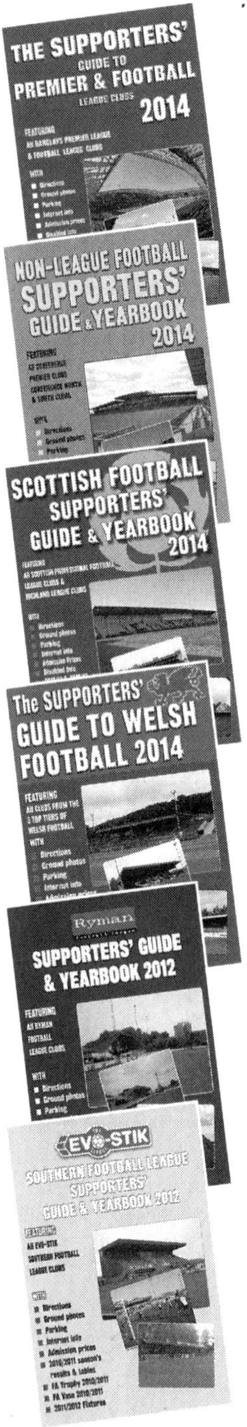

This top-selling series has been published since 1982 and the new 2014 editions contain the 2012/2013 Season's results and tables, Directions, Photographs, Telephone numbers, Parking information, Admission details, Disabled information and much more.

The Supporters' Guide to Premier & Football League Clubs 2014

This 30th edition covers all 92 Premiership and Football League clubs. ***Price £7.99***

Non-League Supporters' Guide and Yearbook 2014

This 22nd edition covers all 68 clubs in Step 1 & Step 2 of Non-League football – the Football Conference National, Conference North and Conference South. ***Price £7.99***

Scottish Football Supporters' Guide and Yearbook 2014

The 21st edition featuring all Scottish Professional Football League and Highland League clubs. ***Price £7.99***

The Supporters' Guide to Welsh Football 2014

The 13th edition covers the 112+ clubs which make up the top 3 tiers of Welsh Football. ***Price £7.99***

Ryman Football League Supporters' Guide and Yearbook 2012

The 2nd edition features the 66 clubs which made up the 3 divisions of the Isthmian League during the 2011/12 season. ***Price £6.99***

Evo-Stik Southern Football League Supporters' Guide and Yearbook 2012

This 2nd edition features the 66 clubs which made up the 3 divisions of the Southern League during the 2011/12 season. ***Price £6.99***

These books are available UK & Surface post free from –

Soccer Books Limited (Dept. SBL)
72 St. Peter's Avenue
Cleethorpes, DN35 8HU
United Kingdom